THE AMAZING ARMADILLO

THE AMAZING ARMADILLO
Geography of a Folk Critter
by Larry L. Smith and Robin W. Doughty

UNIVERSITY OF TEXAS PRESS, AUSTIN

Illustrations by Charles Shaw

First edition, 1984

Requests for permission to reproduce material
from this work should be sent to:
 Permissions
 University of Texas Press
 Box 7819
 Austin, Texas 78713

LIBRARY OF CONGRESS CATALOGING IN PUBLICATION DATA
Smith, Larry Lane.
 The amazing armadillo.
 Bibliography: p.
 1. Nine-banded armadillo. 2. Armadillos. I. Doughty,
Robin W. II. Title.
QL737.E23S64 1984 599.3'1 84-7444
ISBN 0-292-70375-9

Contents

CONTENTS

MAPS

Introduction

Landscapes and the assemblage of plants and animals that give them distinction are in constant flux. Earthquakes, tornadoes, and other natural hazards cause sudden alterations to the face of the earth. Human alterations are far more extensive and varied, sometimes conspicuous, sometimes subtle. The appearance of farms and growth of cities represent the unique powers of humans to alter environments over the long term.

Animals and plants continually change their ranges and numbers and demonstrate the inherently dynamic character of biotic assemblages. "Specialist" organisms, that is, ones having narrow and well-defined food preferences, reproductive behavior, or other activities, may disappear in human-altered landscapes. "Generalist" organisms able to exploit disrupted habitats may replace them.

The "English" or house sparrow and European starling are well-studied examples of birds that have benefited from transport and release by humans. The cattle egret and collared dove have expanded their ranges by occupying the habitats created by agriculture and settlement.[1] Similarly, deer, rabbits, foxes, and cats are among the scores of different mammals that have thrived in disturbed landscapes. North America's coyote, for example, has lived up to a reputation for being cunning and elusive and becoming widespread and numerous despite prolonged efforts to destroy it.

The nine-banded armadillo is another generalist mammal that has vigorously expanded its range and numbers during the past century. This oddity among North American mammals flourishes within the United States, although it arrived here less than 150 years ago with no fanfare and little comment. It has achieved no status as a game animal whose trophy or meat is highly esteemed, and there is little to celebrate about its appearance, movements, bearing, size, or coloration. Yet there is a keen and sizable interest in the armadillo, especially in Texas, its first home state. This book defines that interest, and also traces the vicissitudes of public opinion that first judged it to be more harmful than beneficial.

By 1900, this mobile and adaptable mammal had captured the interest of entrepreneurs who promoted armadillo "shell-baskets" as curios. Scientists specializing in genetic and medical research began to conduct extensive tests on the armadillo. In the last fifteen or twenty years, more and more Texans have increased their regard for this odd-looking mammal. Some lawmakers have described it as having human qualities. It is a "true Texan," they say, tough, pioneering, adaptable, and it generously shares its habitation with others.

This book is about the perception and use of wild animals. It is important to document how attitudes toward animals change as people become interested in and familiar with their life histories and habits. In this sense, our book builds upon the earlier monograph by Edward R. Kalmbach, *The Armadillo: Its Relation to Agriculture and Game*, published by the Texas Game, Fish and Oyster Commission in 1943. Kalmbach's text looked closely at the economic significance of the nine-banded armadillo as a menace to crops and to ground-nesting game birds. Today's public has expressed affection for this mammal, not simply because it consumes injurious insects and benefits medical research. The intangible qualities of the armadillo that we tend to express in terms such as "resourceful," "generous," and "humble" are worth consideration because they reflect, albeit unconsciously, the values that we place on this species and other animals. Such interests and affections color our judgments about preserving or managing them.

This book is also about what the noted ecologist Charles Elton calls "ecological explosions." His classic book, *The Ecology of Invasions by Animals and Plants*, focuses on the enormous increase in numbers of different organisms. We hear a great deal about animals under pressure, that is, threatened with extinction, but it is worth noting that numerical increases and expansions of range are also commonplace. The armadillo exemplifies an "ecological explosion" in the United States. We tend to ignore or disregard similar events because pests to forest products, or other undesirable animals such as alien species that flourish without natural predators, exemplify explosions that we could do well without.

The armadillo is an ecological success story. It is neither an important pest nor an animal that has relied exclusively on humans for transport and release. It continues to occupy new range in the American South. And from what we know, much of this expansion is due to the animal's pioneering abilities. The armadillo prospers in changed environments. It constructs dens in brush-filled fields that cattle have overgrazed, and it feeds in suburban gardens and parks. It is true that people have given a fillip to its colonizing ability by shipping armadillos around the country. But, as in the case of the cattle egret, the precise significance of humans in the mammal's overall distribution is difficult to determine. The armadillo's abilities to adapt, colonize, and increase are evident.

Finally, this book is a contribution to a well-established research theme in geography, namely human activities in exploiting, conserving, and transporting organisms on the face of the earth. A considerable body of literature in American geography exists on animal-related topics, such as animals' role in traditional societies and the economic, ecological, and public health problems associated with native and introduced species. We shall examine these problems and try to explain the factors responsible for the armadillo's distribution and spread, the barriers to its dispersal, and its integration into folklore and popular culture.

Chapter 1 examines the biology and life history of the nine-banded armadillo, which differs from the twenty or so similar species in its expanding range and numbers. Chapter 2 discusses the animal's movements and the history of its spread in the United States, a pattern of distribution that widens annually. Chapter 3 reviews the treatment of this unique animal as a pest and predator. Negative judgments about the harm to game birds and crops changed after field research demonstrated that the armadillo's food preferences were economically more beneficial than harmful. People became interested in keeping armadillos as unusual pets and in decorating their homes with baskets made from their shells. This chapter also describes the current medical research with armadillos that aims to develop a vaccine against Hansen's Disease, or leprosy.

Chapter 4 demonstrates how the growing interest in armadillos—watching them race, tasting their meat in festive cookoffs and barbecues—has enlarged the public's knowledge about the animal. Younger people have come to identify this harmless creature with a relaxed way of living exemplified by progressive country music. Consequently, musicians and artists and larger commercial interests have promoted this "pocket dinosaur" as a symbol of Texas and Texas living. The Lone Star origin of this fad for armadilliana has expanded to other urban centers across the nation, and more and more Americans are familiar with this addition to America's native fauna.

Thanks are due to the many people who responded to a questionnaire that we mailed to more than 140 biologists and state officials in 1978, and to an additional 80 in 1981. We are indebted to experts with Texas Parks and Wildlife and with other wildlife agencies in the South who supplied information and answered our questions about the status and behavior of armadillos. We especially value information or comments from Jerry Cain, Frank Carl, L. Tuffly Ellis, Alan Friedman, Richard Jachowski, Kathryn Apelt Jorns, Valgene Lehmann, Sam Lewis, Nancy Neff, Floyd Potter, Gerald P. Walsh (whose expertise was particularly helpful in writing the section on leprosy), and Frank Weaker.

Archival materials from the Smithsonian Institution proved invaluable, and archivist Renée Jaussaud offered expert guidance to U.S. Fish and Wildlife materials in the National Archives in Washington, D.C. Staff members in the Barker History Center and the Humanities Research Center at the University of Texas at Austin were most cooperative. Personnel from the *Daily Texan* and *Austin-American Statesman* supplied illustrative materials.

Beverly Beaty-Benadom, Amy Bledsoe, Ingrid Dierlam, Alexa Mayer, and Jan Arnold typed drafts of the manuscript, a service for which we are most grateful.

THE AMAZING ARMADILLO

1. The Natural History of Armadillos

Armadillos are members of the animal order Edentata, incorrectly designated as "toothless." They are an ancient and primitive group of mammals that probably originated in North America and migrated to South America before about sixty-five million years ago when the Isthmus of Panama, the corridor connecting the two continents, submerged.

Freed from competition with North American animals, this group of mammals, which currently consists of anteaters, tree sloths, and armadillos, developed and evolved rapidly. Fossil remains of Dasypodidae, the only surviving family of armadillos, are known from the Paleocene epoch, sixty million or so years ago. Other primitive creatures included huge ground sloths, giant armadillos, and glyptodonts—big armadillo-like creatures. These giants moved northward into North America during late Pliocene times a few million years ago when North and South America were connected once again. By the end of the most recent Ice Age, however, the larger edentates had disappeared entirely, although remains of them have turned up in different places, including Texas and Florida. Only their smaller, less specialized cousins remain.[1]

The term *edentate* means "without teeth." However, among modern members of this animal order, only the anteaters are, in fact, toothless. Tree sloths have a few jaw teeth, and all armadillos have primitive peg-like teeth. One species, the giant armadillo, has as many as one hundred teeth, one of the largest numbers in a mammal. Armadillos are the most primitive of the edentates; their neocortex is quite small, but the olfactory brain is well developed and provides a keen sense of smell.[2]

The name *armadillo* comes from the Spanish and means "little armored one," referring to the plate-like shell covering which is unique among mammals. This tough, armored shell, or carapace, which accounts for about 16 percent of body weight, really consists of modified skin tissue and only superficially resembles the exoskeleton of crustaceans or the turtle's shell.

This strange-looking mammal puzzled Swedish botanist Carolus Linnaeus (1707–1778), who, in 1758, coined *Dasypus* as its generic name. This term is derived from the Greek word for "hare" or "rabbit," and reflects that great scholar's attempt to Latinize the Aztec name for the armadillo, *azotochtli*, meaning "tortoise or turtle-rabbit." In combining *novem*, "nine" with *cinctus*, "band or girdle," Linnaeus, who classified plants and animals by using a double name, established the species name *novemcinctus* or "nine-banded." Hence we have *Dasypus novemcinctus*, or the "nine-banded rabbit-turtle."[3]

THE ARMADILLO FAMILY

The family of armadillos, Dasypodidae, is made up of nine genera and approximately twenty species (see Table 1). All of these except the nine-banded armadillo, which is the most widespread of all the edentates, are restricted to Central and South America. They generally inhabit brush-dotted grasslands and wooded places. A few species are found in the hot, moist equatorial lowlands and along the margins of evergreen rainforests. Other armadillos dwell in the uplands of the Andean cordillera, and in the cold, dry desert of Patagonia (see Map 1).

Members of the genus *Tolypeutes*, or three-banded armadillos, of which there are two species, have the unusual ability to curl up into a ball and completely enclose their bodies

TABLE 1. The Armadillo Family

Genus Species	Common Name(s)	Length (in.) (Head + Body) (Tail)	Weight (lbs.)	Range
Tolypeutes				
T. matacus	Three-banded	17.5	—	Bolivia
T. tricinctus	armadillos	3.5		Brazil
				Paraguay
				Argentina
Chaetophractus				
C. nationi	Hairy	8.8–11.2	6	Bolivia
C. vellerosus	armadillos	4.0		Chile
C. villosus	Peludos			Argentina
				Uruguay
Euphractus				
E. sexcinctus	Six-banded	16.5	8–10	East of the
	armadillo	8–10.4		Andes, south to
				southern
				Argentina;
				north to central
				Brazil
Cabassous				
C. centralis	Naked-tailed	12–28	3.3–6.6	East of the
C. hispidus	armadillos	4–7.2		Andes, northern
C. loricatus				Argentina to
C. tatonay				Colombia;
C. unicinctus				Central America
				(*C. centralis*
				only)
Zaedyus				
Z. pichiy	Pygmy	16	2.5–4.5	Argentina
	armadillo	6		Chile
	Pichi			
Chlamyphorus				
C. truncatus	Pink fairy	5–6	0.35	West-central
	armadillo			Argentina
Burmeisteria				
B. retusa	Burmeister's	5.6–7	0.5	South-central
	armadillo	1.4		Bolivia, north-
				ern Argentina
Priodontes				
P. giganteus	Giant	30–40	110–132	Eastern South
	armadillo	20		America

TABLE 1. The Armadillo Family (*continued*)

Genus Species	Common Name(s)	Length (in.) (Head + Body) (Tail)	Weight (lbs.)	Range
Dasypus				
D. kappleri	Kappler's armadillo	22 16	17.5	Surinam Eastern Ecuador Eastern Peru (rare)
D. pilosus	Hairy long-nosed armadillo	14.8–16 10	—	Eastern Ecuador Eastern Peru (very rare)
D. septemcinctus	Seven-banded armadillo	10.6 5.8	3	Eastern Brazil (rare)
D. sabanicola	Northern long-nosed armadillo	11.6 7.8	2.2–4.4	Venezuela Colombia
D. hybridus	Southern long-nosed armadillo	11.8 6.7	4.4	Paraguay Brazil Argentina
D. novemcinctus	Nine-banded armadillo	14.8–17.2 9.8–14.8	7.9–17	(See Figure 1)

SOURCES: Ernest P. Walker, *Mammals of the World*, 3d ed., vol. I; Walburga Moeller, "Edentates," in *Grzimek's Animal Life Encyclopedia*, vol. II; Ralph M. Wetzel and Edgardo Mondolfi, "The Subgenera and Species of Long-Nosed Armadillos, Genus *Dasypus* L.," in *Vertebrate Ecology in the Northern Neotropics*, ed. John F. Eisenberg, pp. 43–63.

within protective shells. In this position, the animal approximates the size of a large, orange or beige-colored grapefruit, and is often called the "little ball" or *bolita* in Spanish. This same defensive posture has occasionally been attributed to the nine-banded armadillo. The nine-banded armadillo, however, is not able to fully bury its lower body in its armor, nor can it roll up into an actual ball; it usually depends upon bursts of speed or frantic burrowing to escape from enemies.

Three-banded armadillos of the species *T. tricinctus* occur in northeastern and central Brazil. The more numerous of the two species, *T. matacus*, also inhabits Bolivia, Paraguay, southwestern Brazil, and northern Argentina, where it is regularly hunted as food. In the wild, the diet of three-banded armadillos consists chiefly of ants and termites, although in captivity they consume fruits, vegetables, bread, and leaves in addition to ants and termites. One captive specimen survived for more than ten years, and others have lived for seven or more.[4]

The genus *Chaetophractus*, or hairy armadillos, has three species: *C. nationi*, *C. vellerosus*, and *C. villosus*. The common name reflects the fact that these armadillos have more body hair than other species. Short, bristly hairs project from the animal's armor, and its belly and legs are covered with longer, light-brown hair. Hairy armadillos, or "peludos" as they are also called, are most common in Argentina; but all three species also occur in Bolivia, Chile, and Uruguay. Peludos feed on insects and grubs, some of which they extract from the rotting carcasses of dead animals. People have also claimed that hairy armadillos attack and kill snakes.

Aridity-adapted *C. vellerosus* dwells in Argentina's southern Monte Desert, where precipitation averages 5.2 inches (130 millimeters) annually, and which has certain floristic and physiographic similarities to the Sonoran Desert in North America. Experiments with this desert armadillo have demonstrated that its kidneys are unusually efficient, a capacity that our familiar nine-banded species lacks. Although this Argentine armadillo would probably prosper in the northern hemisphere's Sonoran Zone, the nine-banded armadillo that has become a permanent resident in the United States cannot do without succulent foods and water, and both of these resources are not always available in the deserts of the U.S. Southwest.[5]

Hairy armadillos are prolific burrowers, and agriculturalists accuse them of causing considerable damage to fields and rangelands, so that these armadillos are frequently the subject of pest control measures. They are also hunted as food, as their flesh is reportedly delicious.[6]

The six-banded armadillo, *Euphractus sexinctus*, is closely related to the hairy armadillos; in parts of Latin America people also call it the "hairy armadillo." Six-banded armadillos are fairly plentiful in several countries of South Amer-

	D. novemcinctus
	D. sabanicola
	D. kappleri
	D. pilosus
	D. septemcinctus
	D. hybridus

MAP 1. Estimated ranges of armadillos in the genus *Dasypus*.

ica east of the Andes, and especially in Brazil. As they are fond of corn and young, tender plants and are expert diggers, they have become a serious menace to croplands. In certain corn-growing regions, people trap six-banded armadillos by leading a trail of corn bait to barrels sunk in the ground into which armadillos topple and from which they cannot extricate themselves.[7]

Another genus, *Cabassous*, has four or five species of so-called "naked-tailed armadillos." They get that name because they lack the protective "armor" on this appendage. They are also called eleven-banded armadillos, but the number of bands varies from ten to thirteen.

Like the six-banded species, naked-tailed armadillos are found east of the Andes from about northern Argentina and Paraguay northward to Colombia. One species, *C. centralis*, also spreads into Central America from Panama into Honduras. Although they are more widely distributed than most other genera of South American armadillos, naked-tailed armadillos are not numerous. They are almost exclusively insectivorous, and dig burrows at the base of termite mounds. They are no threat to crops; and as their flesh is not considered especially tasty, they are not hunted much.

The pygmy armadillo, or "pichi," *Zaedyus pichiy*, which is hunted for its flesh, is abundant throughout much of Argentina, where residents sometimes keep this kitten-sized armadillo as a house pet. It has been introduced into Chile. In cold southern Patagonia, this species is reported to be able to hibernate in winter.[8]

The pink fairy armadillo, *Chlamyphorus truncatus*, is the smallest of all armadillos. It is probably the most specialized and is one of the most unusual in appearance, looking like a small guinea pig with pink armor over its head and back. This armadillo is extremely rare, and its range is restricted to the dry, thorn scrub desert region of west-central Argentina. Burmeister's armadillo, *Burmeisteria retusa*, is closely related to the pink fairy armadillo, but is slightly larger in

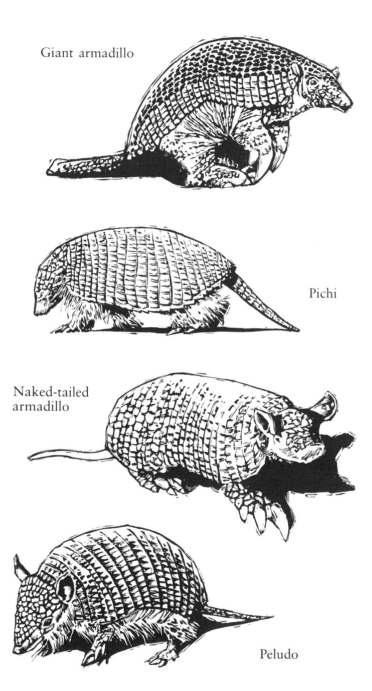

Giant armadillo

Pichi

Naked-tailed armadillo

Peludo

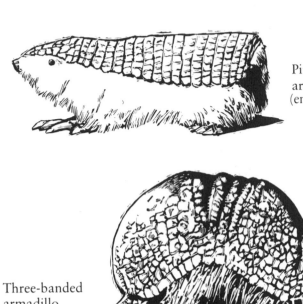

Pink fairy
armadillo
(endangered)

Three-banded
armadillo

Six-banded
armadillo

Nine-banded
armadillo

size and is more widespread. The species also occupies the drylands of Argentina and occurs northward into south-central Bolivia, but is not common. Little is known about the life histories and habits of these two small armadillos. One specimen survived four years in captivity, but other individuals have lived only a few months.[9]

At the other end of the scale of size is the giant armadillo, *Priodontes giganteus*. Compared with other armadillos, it is huge and monster-like, being more than 4 feet in length from head to tail and weighing as much as 132 pounds. Although it is large, the giant armadillo was dwarfed by its distant ancestors, the extinct giant edentates of the Tertiary period.

The giant armadillo inhabits most of eastern South America. It is an active digger, constructing large underground dens, and it plows up the ground in search of insect foods. The diet of giant armadillos consists chiefly of termites and ants, but they also eat a wide variety of spiders, snakes, and carrion. Residents claim the animals will even burrow into newly filled graves, so that in some parts of their range they, as well as other armadillos such as the nine-banded species, are known as "grave diggers."

The giant's considerable size and practice of aggressive digging often cause damage to crops; however, it is not regarded as a serious agricultural pest. Giant armadillos are not hunted regularly as food, but natives in Bolivia eat them occasionally and use their shells for containers.[10]

The best known genus, *Dasypus*, is comprised of six species, namely: *D. kappleri*, Kappler's armadillo; *D. pilosus*, sometimes incorrectly called a hairy armadillo; *D. septemcinctus*, the seven-banded armadillo; *D. sabanicola*, the northern long-nosed armadillo; *D. hybridus*, the southern long-nosed armadillo; and, most important for our purposes, *Dasypus novemcinctus*, the nine-banded armadillo.

Kappler's armadillo has been reported from Surinam on the northeast coast of South America and from the highlands of eastern Ecuador and Peru. These geographically isolated localities may well hold two distinct species. The seven-banded armadillo inhabits the uplands of eastern Brazil, and *D. pilosus* is restricted to a small area in eastern Ecuador and Peru where it overlaps with *D. kappleri*. These three species are not common anywhere; in fact, *D. pilosus* is believed to be very rare. Despite the common names of northern and southern long-nosed armadillos, the *sabanicola* and *hybridus* species do not have the most northerly nor most southerly distribution among armadillos, and both of them have been described only recently. *D. sabanicola* occurs in parts of Venezuela and Colombia, while *D. hybridus* is recorded from eastern Paraguay, northern Argentina, and southern Brazil (see Map 1).[11]

On the other hand, the nine-banded armadillo, *Dasypus novemcinctus*, is probably the most numerous and widely distributed of all armadillos. It exists from northern Argentina through the South American continent east of the Andes, northward into Central America, and is widespread in southern and central Mexico, where it is common. For at least 130 years this species has extended its range in North America by crossing into South Texas and pushing onward both to the north and to the east. This movement is continuing.

The nine-banded armadillo is a stocky, medium-sized animal. Its overall length is about 2.5 feet (61–76 centimeters), and adults weigh about 14 pounds (between 3.6 and 7.7 kilograms). The male is generally slightly larger and heavier than the female. Upper parts are covered with a series of hard plates, covered by a leathery skin, that combine to form the "shell" that is the distinctive feature of all armadillos. The shell has three main parts; a scapular shield over the animal's shoulders, a pelvic shield over the hips, and eight to eleven (but normally nine) transverse bands that join the shields together. These bands are not rigid, but are connected by folds in the skin which allow the armadillo to bend its body a bit like an accordion. The top of the head

11

has tough scales, and the tapering tail is protected by twelve to fifteen rings. The nine-banded armadillo is not flexible enough to completely roll up into a ball as the three-banded armadillo does, but if cornered some individuals may attempt to curl up, thereby protecting their softer, vulnerable underparts. Usually, they depend upon sudden bursts of speed, especially through thorny vegetation, to keep them clear of pursuers. Some may dig ferociously into the soil and cling very tenaciously to the cavity that they have created. The speed at which armadillos may sink themselves into the ground depends on strong, thick legs which are connected to four toes on the forefeet and to five toes on the hindfeet. The toes have wicked-looking curved claws that facilitate rapid digging. In open fields a human can outrun and capture an armadillo, but in heavy brush few people or predatory animals can match its skittering course.[12]

The animal's soft underbelly is not protected by its armor, and hair on its belly is sparse and very fine in texture. The epidermal covering of the head, ears, and legs is much tougher and leathery. The nine-banded armadillo is dull and plain-looking in color, varying from dark brown to light or gray-brown.

FOOD HABITS

Wild nine-banded armadillos are basically insectivorous. However, earthworms, crayfish, small reptiles, amphibians, and even dead birds may be devoured as the animal comes across them. Plant materials account for only a very small percentage of the animal's diet, and much of that may be ingested while foraging for invertebrates. According to Texas folklore, armadillos are said to kill and eat snakes, and they have reportedly been introduced to eastern parts of the state for that purpose. Two wildlife biologists noted that a wild armadillo killed and consumed three young cottontails. Texas folklorist and nature writer J. Frank Dobie reported that someone near Austin had witnessed an armadillo killing five newborn rabbits for the curdled milk in their stomachs. Killing vertebrates, however, seems to be an unusual occurrence.[13]

Armadillos have also been accused of feeding on the eggs of ground-nesting birds, digging up grains, and destroying melon and tomato crops. Extensive research carried out in Texas during the 1930s and 1940s demonstrated that wild armadillos show little interest in birds' eggs. Without well-developed teeth, they find them hard to crack, although they will break them by pushing them against hard objects. While some nests may be damaged and their contents scattered or broken as animals search for other foods, most evidence suggests that declines in game bird populations were not attributable to armadillo predation.[14] Yet, today in parts of South Texas where armadillos are not common, people still hold them responsible for both crop damage and game bird predation. The armadillo's primitive molars are not well adapted for gnawing, chewing, or cracking hard objects. The animal, however, will eat melons or soft fruits, especially if the crop is overripe or has been split open.

DENS, BURROWS, AND HOME RANGES

Nine-banded armadillo burrows and dens come in various shapes and sizes, and serve as shelters and nurseries. Short burrows, often only 12–18 inches long, serve as places of safety. An armadillo usually has a pretty good sense of where safe burrows are located and is normally not very far away from one, but in a pinch it will hastily dig an emergency shelter. Within their home ranges, individual animals frequently have several "active" dens as well as a number of "abandoned" burrows. These permanent shelters may simply consist of one long tunnel terminating in a single nest chamber; or they may be more elaborate, with several entrances leading through side burrows to join in a central den.

A study of burrows constructed in Central Texas showed

that most of them had a single entrance facing to the south. However, burrows with two, three, or four openings oriented to different points of the compass were discovered. Zoology student William K. Clark excavated and took measurements from twenty-six of them. His study revealed that on average the entrance was almost 7 inches in diameter. The length of the tunnels or burrows averaged a little more than 4 feet, ranging from 10 inches to 15 feet. The nest chamber was 13.5 inches in diameter.[15]

Most of the active burrows were located in the banks of streams or in limestone cliffs near surface water supplies which, due to drought in 1947 and 1948, when Clark made his survey, were increasingly hard to find around Austin. Interestingly, Clark discovered that half of the burrows contained nesting chambers. These nesting tunnels averaged about 6 feet long, and each one had a gradual turn in its descent into the ground, in order "to give darkness" for the young, thought Clark.[16]

The nest cavity of the nine-banded armadillo is usually 3–5 feet below the ground surface and is lined with leaves, grass, and other plant debris. A researcher who studied zoo-held armadillos described how individuals collected straw for their nests. An armadillo would bunch straw under its body, then incline on its hindlegs and, with the forepaws clutching the material, would hop, usually backward, to its nest box. By this method, vegetation was collected rapidly and smoothly. Clark witnessed a similar behavior in his study of wild nine-banded armadillos. He saw a female clutch a bundle of oak leaves, grasses, and a few twigs and make off with them to her den. Armadillos change and replenish these insulating materials.[17]

Another interesting aspect about armadillo burrows and nests is the number and types of insects and spiders that are attracted to them (presumably because of their ideal temperature and humidity, much the same as in the crawl space under a house). Spiders, mites, and "thousands" of camel crickets were found in some burrows in central Texas; mosquitoes were present, and the black-widow spider was "a common inhabitant." It is conjectured that resident armadillos feed on these invertebrates, which would be most needed during inclement weather.[18]

In 1977, research was published on the home range of armadillos in south-central Florida. It complemented Clark's work in central Texas almost thirty years earlier. The word "circumscribed" best describes the armadillo's normal living space. Armadillos do not require much room for their everyday activities. The Florida study turned up home ranges of 2.5–35 acres (1–14 hectares) each; most were several hectares in total area. A creature that subsists mainly on ground-dwelling insects usually found in very high densities per unit area does not need to forage over long distances to capture enough to eat, nor does it need to be strongly territorial or aggressive with other individuals of the same species. Working with forty-seven armadillos, the Florida researchers noted little antagonism between individuals, whose home ranges often overlapped.[19]

Permitting the luxury of a little anthropocentrism, we can also observe that our favorite animal is generous. Biologists and others have extracted or scared smaller mammals such as opossums, striped skunks, cotton rats, and burrowing owls from unoccupied armadillo burrows in North America. One correspondent from Victoria County, Texas, notified Vernon Bailey in 1915 that he had captured a pregnant female armadillo who was "sharing" her burrow with a 4-foot-long rattlesnake and a half-grown cottontail—both animals were in side chambers "in the den of this armadillo."[20] This example of sharing has not been lost on the counter-culture folk who have promoted the recent armadillo fad.

REPRODUCTION AND LONGEVITY

Among the twenty or so species of armadillos, reproduction has been closely studied only in the nine-banded species. Mating occurs as early as July or as late as December. William B. Davis has suggested that older, experienced females mate first, followed by younger ones later in the year. The age and sex structure of breeding armadillos as well as local climatic conditions probably influence the timing and duration of the mating season.[21]

Implantation of the fertilized egg may be delayed for up to fourteen weeks after conception. Following implantation in the uterus, four sexually identical embryos develop from the single fertilized egg. Normally, the gestation period is about 150 days, but a recent report indicates that it may be much longer.[22] In spring, usually in March or April, after the colder weather has normally moderated, the female armadillo gives birth to four identical, fully developed young. Young armadillos may be dropped as early as February in more southerly parts of the animal's range in the United States, or as late as May in such northern parts as Arkansas and Oklahoma. Armadillos are born with their eyes open and begin to move about within a few hours. Their pinkish shell is leathery and pliable at first, but in a few days it turns a gray-brown color and begins to harden, although this process is not completed until the animal reaches its full size.

Young armadillos stay with their mother during the spring and summer, emerging from their dens to forage in the evening and night hours. Then, with the onset of the next breeding season, the yearlings are on their own. Although they are neither fully grown nor sexually mature, these immature animals are able to fend for themselves. Sexual maturity is achieved during the animal's second year.[23]

Estimates of the armadillo's life span in the wild vary from four to seven years. In captivity, some animals have survived, and in rare cases reproduced, for up to ten years.[24]

ENEMIES

In early discussions about the spread of the armadillo, several authors suggested that the elimination of carnivorous wolves, coyotes, bobcats, and cougars in South and Central Texas permitted armadillo populations to increase so that animals spread into new territories. Several authorities have argued that successful efforts to poison and trap predatory canids and felines removed an important factor that limited the armadillo's survival. One group of biologists declared that "the most important effect of human settlement was the reduction or extermination of large carnivores . . . which might have provided an effective check on the increase or spread of the armadillo."[25]

In commentaries about enemies other than humans, other writers have maintained that there is no hard evidence that armadillo populations have been affected much by these predators either in Mexico or in Texas. What proof, they asked, did people have that the large carnivores preyed heavily on nine-banded armadillos?[26]

One study of the stomach contents of 569 coyotes in Texas failed to discover the remains of any armadillos. Another one from Oklahoma reported that identifiable remains were present in less than 1 percent of more than 130 coyote stomachs.[27] It is also worth recalling that in 1896, when the famous Harvard-based mammalogist Joel Asaph Allen stated that large predatory animals were widespread in South Texas, the armadillo was building up numbers and spreading in that same area. Allen's list contained the coyote, gray wolf, and bobcat. All of them, he said, were common in the brush country south of San Antonio. Two other cats, the jaguar and ocelot, which are today very rare indeed, were also present, particularly between the Nueces River and the Rio Grande.[28]

Valgene W. Lehmann also lends support to the proposition that natural enemies failed to keep armadillos in check in the latter half of the nineteenth century. In his comprehensive examination of sheep ranching on the South Texas Plain after 1850, biologist Lehmann noted that the "principal wild predators in the Rio Grande Plain during the great sheep era were wolves (probably gray wolves), coyotes, bobcats, mountain lions, and stray dogs." According to Lehmann, bobcats were very common and caused as much trouble as coyotes and wolves. Feral dogs made inroads into sheep herds as well, and efforts to control such predators, even with bounty payments, proved to be initially ineffective. All of the predators that Lehmann said were common in South Texas were also able to feast on armadillos.[29]

Today, campaigns have been waged against these predators for eighty or more years, the armadillo has fewer natural enemies than it had in those years. The wolves have gone, mountain lion numbers have dropped, and pressure remains on bobcats and coyotes. With less predation, therefore, it seems logical to expect that armadillos would become more abundant. But, in fact, in the days when large predators were more numerous, armadillo numbers were increasing, and armadillos were extending their range more rapidly then than in recent years.

The relationship between predator and prey numbers is difficult to analyze because there are no reliable estimates of armadillo populations in South Texas during the nineteenth century. Initially, at least, armadillos must have been exceedingly rare, since early records about land and life in Texas make no mention of them. Later, as ranchers and others moved into Texas, pushing the frontier of settlement from east to west, they encountered armadillos more often. At least part of the apparent increase in armadillo populations and range extension must be attributed to a larger number of people noticing and reporting them.

Coyotes and dogs continue to be regarded as the most important killers of armadillos. A 1974 Texas Parks and Wildlife Department survey lumped coyote and dog predation together, but added that "there were no definite sightings of coyote predation, only assumptions that since some dogs kill armadillos the coyote also does." Another report listed the coyote, black bear, bobcat, fox, raccoon, and dog as enemies of the armadillo. Trained dogs, as well as strays, kill armadillos. An observer recalled that "armadillo hounds, canines of uncertain ancestry, often aided by their human masters, frequently unearth and put an end to their prey."[30]

In the last fifty years the automobile seems to have largely replaced these four-footed enemies of the armadillo, as anyone who has traveled along highways in the American South can readily confirm. A 1939 report mentioned seven dead armadillos along a 7-mile stretch of highway in Harris County, Texas. A few years later it was noted that the crushed remains of armadillos were a "common sight on highways and country roads" in central Louisiana. In Texas and in other states inhabited by armadillos, road kills rank high among agents causing mortality.[31]

PIONEERING ABILITY AND HABITAT PREFERENCES

When permanent armadillo populations were established in Texas in the 1850s, they inhabited a region of thorn scrub or chaparral that stretched from Mexico's eastern state of Tamaulipas into the Rio Grande Plain of South Texas. Soon it was clear that the new mammal was not restricted to that brush country. By about 1900, individuals were seen foraging in Central Texas. Armadillos continued to spread throughout the hilly limestone country in the Edwards Plateau north and west of the Balcones escarpment. Conservationist and author Henry P. Attwater reported that they had "greatly extended" their range, preferring "the rough, waste, uncultivated regions chiefly used for cattle, sheep and goat ranches."[32]

In addition to colonizing the Edwards Plateau, this so-called "shell possum" moved up the coast from the "jungles along resacas" where it made badger-like holes, along the Rio Grande. In the 1890s it reached Nueces Bay, but a field agent for the U.S. Department of Agriculture's Division of Economic Ornithology and Mammalogy (later the Bureau of Biological Survey) stated that armadillos "are not known at all east of Edna [in central Jackson County] even by tradition."[33]

That situation changed within two or three decades. By the mid-1920s, the armadillo occupied a wide variety of environments in South, West, and Central Texas. It was moving into the mixed grasslands in north-central parts, and was well established in the alluvial creek and wooded bottom lands from East Texas into Louisiana. It was leaving the transition zone between the tropics and mid-latitudes, and moving into the mixed mesophytic and deciduous forest lands of southeastern North America.

But it is safe to say that the animal was not evenly distributed across its range. Limited data have revealed that the home ranges of individuals vary from about 10 acres (4 hectares) in the Hill Country near Austin, Texas, to 50 acres (20 hectares) around Natchitoches, Louisiana.[34] Another important consideration involves the rate of spread. One authority reports an average invasion rate of about 2.5–6.5 miles (4–10 kilometers) per year "in the absence of obvious physical or climatic barriers." This slow expansion, which has been likened to that of the cotton rat and the masked shrew, reflects the sedentary characteristics of *D. novemcinctus*. However, the low dispersal tendencies of young animals are compensated for by weak homing abilities of individuals, so that when an armadillo finds itself in an unfamiliar environment, it keeps moving in search of favorable habitat.[35]

The armadillo's preference for riparian habitats has enabled it to disperse along river valleys. In times of drought or failing food supplies, individuals are likely to follow dry creek beds in search of pools of water.

Their paths may carry them beyond their normal haunts and result in new colonization. When more favorable conditions return, newcomers or juveniles fill in the areas of previously discontinuous or sparse distribution. Maps showing the range of the armadillo frequently indicate such "pioneering groups" beyond the main area of distribution. In time, groups may grow larger and merge with animals in the main range. New animals then move away and repeat the "leapfrog" effect of range extension.

Places with available water, woody plant cover for shelter and protection, and friable soils containing abundant invertebrate foods are the homes for highest numbers of armadillos. These situations are commonly found in river valleys and near streams, although waterlogged or marshy places are too wet for prolonged occupation.[36]

In semiarid regions of West Texas, for example, armadillos concentrate along streams or water holes, where Bailey saw "perfect prints of the side of the animal's shell," as well as "three toed tracks and the print of its dragging tail" in small, muddy places.[37] The dissected river valleys in Central Texas are good places for armadillos and support larger numbers due, in part, to a ready supply of drinking water and to the natural cavities in the limestone cliffs where animals find refuge. Some armadillos have been found several miles from surface water in West Texas, and one observer has suggested that they may be able to go without drinking water for three or four weeks.[38] Another person, however, discovered that they "drank ravenously" after water was withheld for five days. Armadillos may obtain some of their water requirements from invertebrate foods, but unless surface water is available they do not remain in an area for long.[39]

Vegetation plays a lesser role in the numbers of armadillos an area will support. The animal shows a preference for individual plants rather than for plant species. Cover and protection are its principal requirements, so that it is likely to be attracted by a thicket, a patch of scrub, or a fence-line where suitable crevices, plant roots, or soil afford hiding places. It has been noted that many armadillos in a large tract of brush abandoned it after vegetation was cleared. A wildlife biologist has suggested that brush clearance for cropland has been responsible for local declines in South Texas.[40]

The effect of soil types on an animal with such a large range is difficult to determine. Greatest armadillo population densities occur in Texas in the sandy-clays of the eastern pine belt. The pine and hardwood forest zone of the South provides excellent cover, friable soils, and water, which can support large numbers of animals. Population densities are not so large in the blackland prairie zone of Central Texas, where cotton and grains have replaced most of the native vegetation. And the hard, dry soils of West Texas that do not have large quantities of insects are less attractive for armadillos to exploit.[41]

Nine-banded armadillos have not permanently occupied the barrier islands along the Gulf of Mexico or Atlantic coasts. They have, in general, also avoided low-lying wetlands, places such as Florida's Everglades, where dens and burrows would be easily flooded. In Florida armadillos have a liking for citrus groves and also forage in fields where truck crops are grown. They have been blamed for causing considerable damage by burrowing into irrigation ditches.[42]

In similar croplands in the lower Rio Grande Valley of Texas, however, armadillos are seen only rarely in citrus groves or in fields with vegetable crops. There they seem to prefer to stick close to the relatively few remaining places with uncleared or overgrown brush near the Rio Grande and to the pastures several miles north of that river.

Armadillos may be displaced temporarily from areas under urban expansion, but have adapted to suburban situations. They use golf courses and parks for denning, and the well-watered lawns and gardens in residential neighborhoods as feeding areas.

CLIMATIC BARRIERS TO RANGE EXTENSION

For a long time it has been recognized that the ultimate range of the armadillo is limited by long-term aridity and by extended periods of low temperatures in winter. This statement is true for any number of animal species. Variations in

23

temperature and rainfall bring range extension to a temporary halt. Permanent extremes in one or another climate element may result in sterile areas for armadillos and form a barrier which populations of breeding animals do not cross.[43]

The armadillo is not greatly affected by high summer temperatures because it will adjust its activities to the coolest hours of the day, emerging to feed after dark. Such behavioral adaptations are important, as experiments have demonstrated that when temperatures exceed 100° F the animal's breathing quickens, and it begins to pant and lie on its side in order to facilitate heat loss.

On the other hand, an armadillo is able to tolerate extreme cold better than extreme heat. This statement may, at first glance, appear misleading because the nine-banded species neither stores large quantities of body fat nor, so far as we know, hibernates. Therefore, it would seem that armadillos are susceptible to low temperatures, especially if faced with several consecutive days of subfreezing conditions.[44]

In captivity armadillos have died when the room temperature was reduced to 40° or 50° F for "a day or two" according to Kalmbach; and there are reliable reports that wild armadillos expire in extended periods of extremely cold weather. In one of these, the ground surface was covered with ice and snow; in another case, freezing temperatures persisted for three weeks, dropping periodically below 5° F.[45] Such conditions cut off access to food so that armadillos succumb from a combination of starvation and exposure to cold. Without large reserves of body fat, armadillos were not able to wait out the extended periods of freezing weather, and the need for food prompted them to leave their burrows and become exposed to the very low temperatures.

However, the armadillo has made some behavioral and physiological adjustments that enable it to survive cold. When captive armadillos were exposed to cold, "an animal immediately arose and tucked his head under his belly," noted one observer. This "ball-like" posture was maintained for several hours, as the room temperature was dropped to freezing. Researcher Kjell Johansen saw that armadillos began shivering to help offset cold and showed "an amazing ability to remain crouched in their ball-like posture for hours."[46]

Kathryn Apelt Jorns, who has observed wild and captive armadillos for about forty years, commented that "during some bad winters we saw only a few armadillos, but in the spring they would reappear as if nothing had happened."[47] Professor Frank Weaker has reported similar experiences. Weaker captures armadillos for his medical work from along the Guadalupe River between Kendalia and Sisterdale in Kendall County, Texas. During the winter months he finds few armadillos, but in spring and summer, populations once again appear to be normal and include lots of young animals.[48] Our own observations of armadillos at two locations in Central Texas between 1978 and 1981 also confirm that animals are not very active during the colder months, but more of them are seen once the weather becomes warmer.

One expert has speculated that more northerly-based armadillos give birth in late spring when most cold spells of weather are over.[49] The presence of a resident population in northern Oklahoma and Arkansas supports his position. A burrow or den that attracts insects also provides the inhabitant with an emergency food supply. Replenishment in the type, quantity, and placement of insulating plant materials gives protection from the cold in subterranean dens. However, more information is needed about the mechanisms that enable animals to survive in colder areas.

Very dry conditions prevailing in the Chihuahuan Desert of far West Texas and northern and eastern Mexico have a limiting effect upon the distribution and dispersal of the nine-banded armadillo. It has been noted that aridity "exerts its most suppressive effect through limiting the armadillo's food supply of insects and other invertebrates."[50] The hard, stony desert soils of the American Southwest also make the digging of dens more difficult. The nine-banded armadillo is also physiologically unsuited to arid environments. One important study compared the renal capability of the hairy armadillo with that of the nine-banded armadillo. The hairy armadillo inhabits the Monte of Argentina, a region physiographically similar to the Sonoran Desert in the United States. The study's findings show that the hairy armadillo has the ability to concentrate water in its kidneys and will subsist, at least for part of the year, on *Prosopis* pods (mesquite beans) which have a water content of at least 6 percent. The kidney of the nine-banded armadillo, on the other hand, is not adapted to life in such a xeric environment. Furthermore, vegetable matter usually makes up only a very small percentage of its diet.[51]

Short-term droughts, from a few months to a year or more, have telling effects on armadillos even in areas where they are widespread. In the western and southern parts of Texas these effects can be pronounced. In areas of generally low rainfall (less than 10–12 inches [250–300 millimeters] per year), surface streams do not flow for several months of the year. Surface water impoundments such as stock tanks evaporate, leaving the armadillo without much free surface water. And it is at these times that thirsty armadillos abandon home ranges and go in search of water.[52] Armadillos may be able to survive on water taken in the food they consume, but without drinking water animals become increasingly emaciated. Longer periods of drought decimate them.

Frequent attempts have been made to establish the final outer limits to the animal's range by the intolerance to aridity and cold. Bailey, who compiled the first map of its range in Texas, for instance, suggested that the armadillo was confined to the semiarid brush country in the south, but acknowledged that it occurred much farther north. The belief persisted in later reports that the armadillo's continued spread northward into north-central Texas would be blocked by winter cold. This has not happened.[53]

As armadillos have continued into Oklahoma, Arkansas, and beyond, researchers have become more cautious in attempting to establish an absolute latitudinal limit for their range. From current evidence, it is clear that the armadillo not only is more tolerant of cold weather than was once suspected, but also is better able to cope with winter weather than with drought. It has been suggested that the cold barrier itself may have shifted northward, permitting this mammal to reach beyond the limits set by earlier workers. Supporters of this hypothesis have studied climatic data from 1914 to 1970. These data seem to indicate that the mean annual number of "freeze days" (any day when the maximum temperature is at or below 32° F) in Texas and Oklahoma has declined. A tolerance level of nine freeze days per year has been established for the armadillo. In 1970, this figure placed the winter barrier just north of Oklahoma City.[54] Since that time armadillos (and perhaps the winter cold barrier too) have continued their northward movement.

2. Distribution and Dispersal in the South

Today, the nine-banded armadillo is a common and widespread resident in eight states—Texas, Louisiana, Arkansas, Oklahoma, Alabama, Mississippi, Florida, and Georgia. Animals have been reported from Tennessee and South Carolina, where they are expected to become more common, and occur in certain localities in New Mexico, Kansas, and Missouri, where people rarely see them and where they are not considered to be permanent residents. This pattern of distribution is not the result of a sudden, uniform, and large-scale invasion along a "broad front." It represents gradual advances, periodic stops, and even retreats, according to fluctuating conditions and the need to obtain sufficient food (see Map 3).

Under favorable conditions, the nine-banded armadillo may enlarge its overall range by several hundred square miles in a year. But during drought, floods, or prolonged cold weather, local populations die off or animals move out. On the arid and colder margins of this species' range in the west and north, such hazardous conditions may bring about considerable fluctuations in the area that armadillos occupy.

Most habitats in the central portions of the armadillo's range, for example in Louisiana, southern Arkansas, and eastern Oklahoma, have been colonized during several decades of slow but steady pioneering. East of the Mississippi River, notably in Florida, Georgia, and Alabama, armadillos consolidated a base from which they spread after people released individual animals or others escaped from captivity.

Such human-assisted introductions have given a fillip to the armadillo's natural abilities to establish itself in a wide variety of environments.

It has been suggested that scores, or even hundreds, of armadillos have been introduced into the southeastern United States. Precise information about these introductions is difficult to obtain. Nevertheless, one group of researchers was successful in locating people in Florida and Mississippi who knew of "definite instances of such introductions, and attributed the local populations to such sources."[1] A similar spread by transport and release or escape has taken place in Alabama and has contributed significantly to the extension of the animal's range. People have apparently released armadillos in South Carolina too, but as yet there is no evidence that a resident population exists in that state. The practice of transporting armadillos into new areas is continuing; once a permanent breeding population becomes established, the extent and impact of subsequent introductions is impossible to ascertain.

While recognizing that the distribution of the nine-banded armadillo is an ongoing and fluctuating phenomenon, we have delineated its current range with a line around the outermost limits of the animal's estimated occurrence. Obviously, not all armadillos exist within this line, nor do they occupy all of the area within its borders. Marshlands, for example, are too wet, and grasslands frequently lack sufficient cover for dens. It is also important to remember that armadillos are not distributed evenly in those environments in which they flourish.

INVASION OF TEXAS

Armadillos have been present on the Texas side of the Mexican border in the lower Rio Grande Valley since before the 1850s. Although initial entry appears to have resulted from individuals swimming or literally "walking" across the Rio Grande, it is possible that people carried some of the first armadillos into Texas; it is recorded that animals were kept for food in the Mexican border towns.[2] Benjamin Lundy (1789–1839), who traveled extensively in Texas and northern Mexico on three visits in the early 1830s, saw what was probably a captive armadillo in Matamoros, just across the border from Brownsville, in 1834. Lundy described the armadillo as an "amphibious animal . . . about the size of a muskrat, with a shell and skin resembling in texture those of the alligator, and having wreaths or seams, like those of the rhinoceros, around its body, from the head to the end of the tail. It is a pretty creature, and wonderfully expert at burrowing." In the late 1840s Viktor Bracht (1819–1886), German immigrant and entrepreneur who explored many parts of south-central Texas, noted that armadillos "are found east of the Rio Grande, close to Mexico."[3]

The first detailed account of the new animal in the Lone Star State came in the mid-1850s when famed ornithologist John James Audubon (1785–1851) and John Bachman published information about the mammal in their three-volume work *Quadrupeds of North America*. Their informant, Captain H. P. McGown, who was stationed in the lower Rio Grande Valley, reported that animals existed in the brush or chaparral along the Rio Grande. In addition he described a smaller armadillo, judged to be a second species, which inhabited the more elevated and stony places. Saying that he had come across armadillo shells out "on the prairie," McGown implied that armadillos could be encountered some distance from the river, but he did not know whether these shells came from "habitants or were carried there by birds."[4]

Nine-banded armadillos moved eastward from this first zone of entry between Brownsville and Rio Grande City. Progress was so rapid that by 1880, paleontologist Edward Drinker Cope (1840–1897), who worked for the Geological Survey of Texas, suggested that the mammal had

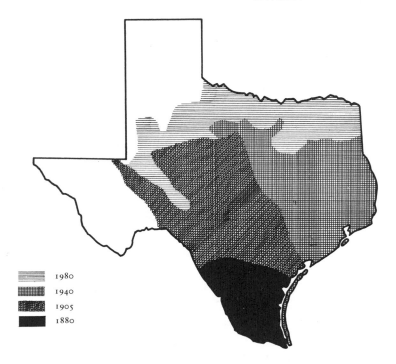

1980
1940
1905
1880

MAP 2. Range extension of the nine-banded armadillo in Texas, 1880–1981.

moved as far north as the Nueces River. Individuals had also spread west to Frio City in semiarid Frio County, which abuts onto the southern edge of the Edwards Plateau (see Map 2).[5]

The outer limit of Cope's estimated range for armadillos passed through Atascosa County, where in January 1879 a woodcutter captured his first animal and sent it to nearby San Antonio to sell. This animal, which the city newspaper announced triumphantly as "the first ever found in Western Texas," was put in a wagon for the citizens to see. Hundreds of people reportedly gathered to view this odd-looking creature whose "proper" home was supposed to be in South America where natives hunted it for food. Readers were assured that armadillos traveled at night searching for "fruits, roots, and insects," and especially ants. It is not known whether the $50 asking price was paid by "some curiosity seeker."[6]

During the next few years armadillos continued to push northward, spreading into the Edwards Plateau and extending into its southeastern section, the so-called Texas Hill Country. Before 1900, people had killed or captured armadillos in Burnet, Kerr, Kendall, and Gillespie counties west of Austin. Additional armadillos inhabited the banks of Onion Creek, a few miles south of the capital city, and others were common toward the coast along the Navidad River in Lavaca County.[7]

Shortly after the turn of the century, Vernon Bailey (1864–1942), who worked as a biologist for the U.S. Department of Agriculture's Bureau of Biological Survey, traveled throughout Texas and collected data about the state's fauna. In October 1905, this Chief Field Naturalist published his "Biological Survey" of lizards, snakes, and mammals in Texas, and included a distribution map in the section about the "Texas Armadillo."[8] In the twenty-five years following Cope's survey, *Dasypus novemcinctus* had made enormous strides in the total area that it occupied in Texas. It resided in virtually all of the brush country, having possibly benefited from the proliferation and spread of cactus and shrubs on the South Texas Plain due to overgrazing by livestock. It had also moved up the river valleys that incised the rugged limestone upland of the Edwards Plateau. Armadillos had even managed to occupy a long, narrow strip of land on both sides of the Pecos River, on what has become the edge of its western range. Bailey reported, however, that it was found infrequently that far west; some people characterized it as present only "occasionally" along the Pecos River, and rarely as far as Langtry.[9]

Vernon Bailey judged the armadillo to be "common" from Matagorda Bay in Calhoun County south to the lower

Rio Grande Valley. He cited an earlier note that "a cowboy saw an armadillo near the center of Padre Island." Its range extended upstream from Brownsville to the Rio Grande's confluence with the Pecos River. East of the Pecos Valley the northern limit of its range followed an uninterrupted line from Martin County to about Breckenridge in Stephens County; then swung southeastward at almost a 90° angle back to Victoria and Calhoun counties, bisecting Williamson and Bastrop counties (see Map 2).[10]

The armadillo inhabited much of western Texas, that is beyond the 98°W meridian of longitude. Within that region armadillos could be found in a semitropical strip along the Gulf Coast, and in the much larger mesquite-dominated South Texas Plain, where rainfall averages less than 30 inches annually. The animal did not seem well adapted to the usually arid conditions in the Panhandle, Llano Estacado, or Trans-Pecos.[11]

Bailey concluded that armadillos were unlikely to move beyond West Texas. They did not occur "as a rule" east of the semiarid mesquite belt, and they ranged to about 33°N latitude.[12] He admitted, however, that some people believed that animals were heading eastward across the 98°W meridian. He was uncertain, however, whether this belief was related to new expansion or to a population build-up in the established range that made animals more conspicuous. The former opinion proved to be true. Bailey's map showed outlying "pockets" of armadillos in Colorado, eastern Washington, and Houston counties, east of the main body of armadillos. Why these animals had progressed so far into this so-called Austroriparian or humid section of the state, Bailey did not say. He described the early presence in Houston County (1899) of an armadillo that "wandered into a smoke house and was caught and kept alive for some time" near Antioch.[13]

One possible explanation rests with humans. The animal in the smokehouse may have had a premonition! Bailey mentioned how folk in the Rio Grande Valley liked armadillo flesh. It is plausible that people carried animals as "meat on the hoof" to communities in interior Texas. A recent book about early life in the Big Thicket of southeast Texas contains an anecdote about a Dr. Lovett who imported armadillos into Liberty County, which is south of Houston County, after the turn of the present century in order to "help control snakes in the cane fields." [14] Armadillos do consume injurious insects, but if the good doctor was expecting a relative of the mongoose, then his animals may well have ended up in the pot. Residents of East Texas have a tradition of consuming armadillos and even feeding an armadillo stew to their cattle, pigs, and chickens. There was nothing to stop them from carrying live animals back to their homes beyond the armadillo's usual range and thereby giving this species, which can quickly dig its way to freedom, a fresh start.

East Texas agrees closely in climate, physiognomy, vegetation, and a large number of plant and animal species with the lower Mississippi River Valley, so that there seemed nothing to stop *D. novemcinctus* from heading off into Louisiana, Mississippi, and beyond, after it had consolidated its foothold in East Texas. Bailey lived to see this accomplishment.

John K. Strecker, curator of Baylor University Museum in Waco, took a keen interest in the changing status of Texas' fauna. He collected information about the armadillo's movements both before and after Bailey's pioneer research, and he traced the animal's continued movement north and east. Strecker reported that some armadillos had migrated into the High Plains above the Caprock escarpment, where Bailey had concluded that conditions were too extreme.

During a visit to Palo Duro Canyon and vicinity in May and June 1910, Strecker noted statements from reliable ranchmen who had seen, killed, or captured armadillos that had entered Armstrong County "since 1905." He argued that "within recent years the range of the armadillo has been greatly extended," and included a single specimen taken near Waco, his home base, in September 1903. But the mammal failed to become established permanently on the High Plains around Palo Duro Canyon. The first individuals that Strecker referred to disappeared; later studies turned up very few. Breeding continues in the Rolling Plains south of the Caprock escarpment, but armadillos are scarce.[15]

Armadillos persisted in low numbers in a tier of counties south of the Red River, especially during the drought of the late 1920s and early 1930s. They began, however, to increase slowly until by the early 1950s infilling of the present range in North Texas was just about completed. In other words, distribution was more or less continuous from the lower Rio Grande Valley to the Red River and from the Pecos River to the Sabine River—an area of approximately 160,000 square miles.

Armadillos inhabit two-thirds of Texas, but are not evenly distributed. Densities are lowest in dry western areas, are higher in moister regions, and peak in riparian environments in central and eastern sections. In recent years armadillo numbers have reportedly dropped in north-central Texas due, it is believed, to the unusually severe winters of 1976–1977 and 1977–1978 and the unusually dry summer of 1978. These extreme conditions also stifled increases in South Texas, where the very dry summer of 1979 has kept numbers at what appears to be a normal level of about one animal per 20 acres (about 8 hectares).[16]

Armadillos have inhabited the lower Pecos River Valley for at least the last decade. Current reports indicate that animals have pushed into the High Plains again, traditionally marginal for permanent occupation. In 1981, biologists and agricultural agents noted them in Childress, Collingsworth, Wheeler, and Hemphill counties, between 34 and 36°N latitude. Individual armadillos have also turned up from time to time, and as recently as 1978, west of the Pecos River, but there seems to be little prospect for them in such a dry region.[17]

A drop in armadillo numbers during the early 1970s along the Rio Grande in Zapata, Starr, Hidalgo, and Cameron counties was probably caused by brush clearance.[18] The face of the lower Valley is changing rapidly as bulldozers flatten large tracts for urban expansion and clear land of indigenous trees and bushes for irrigation agriculture. Armadillos have disappeared from such cleared strips, but remain fairly common in places where scrub vegetation is left intact, for example, on the banks of the Rio Grande and beside creeks, drainage ditches, and older irrigation canals.

RANGE CONSOLIDATION: LOUISIANA, ARKANSAS, AND OKLAHOMA

The nine-banded armadillo first appeared in Louisiana in about 1916 or 1917, when pioneers moved from Texas. During the 1920s, it consolidated a foothold, built up numbers, and spread throughout much of the state, becoming most abundant in the western parishes where it had first appeared. Only wetlands along the Gulf Coast are not occupied by armadillos, whose dens would soon become waterlogged there. In many places animals have become so common that residents regard them as pests.[19]

The first record of armadillos in Arkansas was from Washington County in 1921. During that decade, animals were frequently sighted along the Sabine River south in Texas. It is likely that first Arkansas records were "Texas pioneers" which followed the tributaries of the Sabine, moved into the Red River basin, then crossed into the watershed of the Arkansas River in southwestern and south-central Arkansas. Armadillos spread throughout southern Arkansas and moved into Oklahoma, where they were first reported near Tulsa in 1936. Other animals were seen much farther south near Ardmore in 1939.[20]

The 1940s and early 1950s are characterized by continued range expansion and an increasing number of armadillos in south-central states. By 1954, this species occupied virtually all of southern Arkansas. It was well established in southeastern Oklahoma, too, and a sizable but isolated group of animals inhabited north-central parts of that state. Several smaller pockets were noted north of the main areas of distribution in both Oklahoma and Arkansas.[21]

During the late 1960s and early 1970s, armadillo numbers in southern Arkansas increased dramatically, and individuals crossed into areas north of the Arkansas River. Eight counties had estimates of higher numbers than in 1960. This unprecedented movement was possibly due, in part, to greater interest in armadillos as more people paid attention to their whereabouts and status. On the contrary, reports from Oklahoma for the same period suggested that low population densities prevailed in most counties until at least 1970. At that time armadillos were rare in northern Oklahoma and did not occur in the Panhandle or in other counties adjacent to the Texas Panhandle.[22]

By 1977, Arkansas' armadillos were recorded as "present

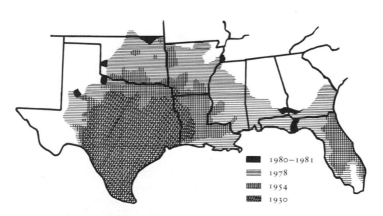

■	1980–1981
≡	1978
▦	1954
▨	1930

MAP 3. Distribution of the nine-banded armadillo in the U.S. South.

and well established in all but the northeast quarter of the state."[23] Currently, population density appears to be highest south of the Arkansas River, and correspondents suggest that numbers remained fairly stable throughout the state from 1977 to 1982. However, some county agents have noted declines in Drew, Hot Springs, and Union counties and attributed them to the bitterly cold winters of 1976–1977 and 1977–1978.

Recent information indicates that the armadillo is now a well-distributed resident throughout the eastern two-thirds of Oklahoma. Population density is lowest in the north and west and increases in the south and southeast. There are some exceptions to this general trend, however. The agent in Washita County, near the western limit of the animal's range, declared that armadillos have "appeared all over the county since 1970, and now they are everywhere."[24] In Payne County, in north-central Oklahoma, armadillos have become more widespread and abundant in the last decade. Armadillos have also increased in Pushmataha County in the southeastern part of the state, where they are now considered a problem because of digging into lawns and gardens.

The range of the armadillo in Oklahoma appears to be limited by increasing aridity in the western and Panhandle sections. There has been some "filling in" of range in the northern half of the state, and numbers there have stabilized or are said to be increasing. In Arkansas, it is probably only a matter of time before armadillos move permanently into the northeastern counties. Nevertheless, their ability to maintain a stable population and flourish in the northern parts of both Arkansas and Oklahoma is likely to depend on the severity of winter weather.

PROGRESS EAST OF THE MISSISSIPPI

The armadillo's first notable success in establishing itself east of the Mississippi River came not as one would expect in eastern Louisiana or western Mississippi but in Florida, where in 1922, a young boy caught one near the city of Miami. He carried the animal to the Miami Beach Zoo, where he met H. H. Bailey, who became curious about the novel creature and traced its origin. From his investigation, Bailey learned that a Marine from Texas who was stationed at Hialeah during World War I had brought a pair of armadillos with him and had released them after the war. A few years later, another pair escaped from a private zoo near Cocoa, and other reports of escapees continued to be recorded until the mid-1940s.[25]

Shortly afterward, people realized that the armadillo had created a well-defined range along the East Coast, with isolated groups of animals breeding inland. By 1960 all of Florida except the Everglades and Panhandle contained armadillos; ten years after that, they were abundant in the western Panhandle. The central Panhandle had no armadillos, so that most of the Florida population remained cut off from armadillos farther west.[26]

As recently as 1974, western and eastern armadillo groups were separated by "a hiatus of 220 km, including two north-south rivers" in the central Panhandle of Florida.[27] Because the armadillo's range in Florida was already well known, we contacted people about its status in the central Panhandle. In 1978, we learned that the gap between the two separate groups had narrowed to about 25 miles (40 kilometers), between the Apalachicola and Ochlockonee rivers. The significance of this divide lessened as it was subsequently discovered that the "bridge" between the armadillos had been completed in southern Georgia (see Map 3). Today, all counties in the Florida Panhandle hold armadillos, but populations remain low in the central region.

Surprisingly, armadillos did not appear in the state of Mississippi until 1928, and their first appearance may well have been due to humans transporting them. Records from a zoo director in Jackson showed that, in about 1934, armadillos were frequently found in railroad cars carrying cattle

39

from Texas. The animals were probably mixed with cattle as a practical joke, but some of them seem to have escaped and reproduced in west-central districts.[28]

By 1950, the nine-banded armadillo had spread from the Jackson area and was well-established throughout the southwestern quarter of Mississippi. However, it took considerable effort to convince State Game and Fish Commission members that the armadillo was there to stay. The commission argued that travelers from Louisiana were "dumping" animals, and therefore, it was not really a resident. At least one report, however, dating back to the early 1950s, included western Mississippi in the armadillo's breeding range, and it had crossed the Mississippi River by 1954.[29]

Less than twenty years later, armadillos were abundant throughout the southern half of Mississippi, where several counties showed increases. People were beginning to consider the new mammal a pest and requested advice about eradicating it. In the mid-1970s, a sizable expansion in range took place in northwestern Mississippi, and our 1978 survey confirmed that the armadillo is now common in all but northeastern Mississippi. Population density is lowest in the north, with less than ten armadillos per 100 acres, and highest in the south. Numbers are increasing. A respondent in Yazoo County, for example, noted declines in places that were being cleared for urban expansion; but five years later, numbers in the same county were on the upswing. We expect the armadillo to occupy the entire state, but population density in the northern counties may lag behind that in southern counties, as cold winters take a toll.[30]

The armadillo is established solidly in southwestern Alabama, where it was probably imported from other areas. There are several reports of releases, and at least one of them (in 1937) near Foley in Baldwin County led to a permanent population. A gravid female was captured in Auburn in 1939; however, that locality does not now appear to favor the species.[31]

The 1978 survey indicated low but stable numbers in Coffee, Geneva, and Houston counties in southeastern Alabama. In January 1981, a half-dozen armadillos were noticed within 35 miles of Montgomery; questionnaire responses show that armadillo numbers in Alabama are on the upswing. Some northward movement is taking place, but there is still no hard evidence of large numbers in central Alabama. No obvious physical or climatic barrier hinders expansion, but the armadillo has not spread as rapidly in Alabama as in other southern states.

Although Georgia's first armadillo record was in 1947, when someone captured one near Decatur, the animal's status remained uncertain until about 1970, when a large and growing population was discovered in Camden County.[32] An extension of range appears to have taken place in southeastern Georgia during the early 1970s, so that currently state and county officials regard the animal as being well established on the coastal plain next to the Florida border.

Our survey turned up the first record of an armadillo from Troup County in western Georgia, and in January 1981, several residents of La Grange, in the same county, said that they see armadillos from time to time but the animals are not numerous.

The dense network of rivers and streams in Georgia provides a pathway for dispersal. Expansion into the coastal plain has been fairly rapid, and current reports indicate that well-established armadillos in the southern part are increasing. This animal may soon become a resident in upland areas too, when one considers the large number of sightings north of the "core" area in Georgia.

OUTLYING RECORDS

Scattered reports of nine-banded armadillos have come from Kansas, New Mexico, and Missouri for a number of years, and a single specimen has been reported from Colorado. Although armadillos are seen on rare occasions in

Kansas and Missouri, they do not appear to have established themselves, as there are no confirmed breeding records. One expert has suggested that these animals die out or fail to find a mate.[33] A possible exception comes from Sumner County in south-central Kansas, which has a history of sightings. In 1978, several armadillos were seen in summer, and road casualties are a regular occurrence. However, there is no evidence that armadillos are reproducing successfully. The few armadillos that people encounter may have wandered north from Oklahoma.

In his 1905 report, Vernon Bailey noted that armadillos had been detected in Loving County, Texas, next to the New Mexico boundary, and his map showed that the animals had crossed the border. But in 1931, in a later publication, he referred to the armadillo's status in New Mexico as, that of "a rare animal on the extreme border of its range."[34] State and county officials who responded to the 1978 survey had not discovered armadillos anywhere. However, two reports from the Pecos River in north-central New Mexico in 1962, and again in early 1970, suggest that it may be a rare visitor.[35]

Armadillo populations along the Texas–New Mexico border are certainly low, and it is improbable that the animal will inhabit New Mexico, due to arid conditions. Wetter than usual circumstances make the Pecos River Valley offer an accessible route into southeastern New Mexico, but breeding on a permanent basis is not favored.

Replies to our survey in Missouri did not mention many armadillos. One respondent recorded a number from southwestern Missouri over several years, and he concluded that some armadillos manage to survive for two or three seasons before succumbing. The species is very unlikely to become a permanent resident.

Prospects look much brighter in Tennessee, where armadillos were first reported in 1974.[36] They were solitary individuals, or "hardy pioneers," that had made the trek from

Arkansas or Mississippi into six or seven southwestern counties. At that time, few animals apparently survived, but a recent note suggests that southwestern Tennessee should now be included in the animal's range.[37]

Records of armadillos occurring in South Carolina have been accumulating slowly since the mid-1960s. State wildlife officials suspect that most desultory reports concerned escaped or released "pets," as most animals were close to major highways which tourists use in traveling from Florida and Georgia.[38] In spite of a growing number of sightings, including road kills, South Carolina wildlife officials do not think that the armadillo is a permanent resident. However, it seems to be only a matter of time before South Carolina is included in the animal's range.

FUTURE TRENDS

In the early years after 1900, biologists and other interested persons thought that the armadillo would not survive much farther north than Dallas, Texas, or about 33°N latitude. By the mid-1950s these curious-looking mammals were common in central Oklahoma and were still pushing northward. Investigators were much more cautious in establishing an absolute northern limit to the armadillo's range.[39] Range extension into the Trans-Pecos across the Sonoran Desert is blocked by a paucity of surface moisture, so there has been less interest in speculating about possible limits in the west. The animal encountered them early.

Recently, however, one expert has suggested that the "moisture barrier" is moving eastward, to be followed by a so-called "range regression" as armadillos abandon drier western areas in Texas.[40]

In the last chapter we discussed the armadillo's sensitivity to cold and its inability to adjust well to desert conditions. Keeping these two environmental constraints in mind, we shall speculate about the ultimate distribution in the South.

Since about 1954, studies have shown that armadillos in

West Texas have responded to drought. In wetter years numbers increase, and in times of drought they decline. But how are these population changes reflected in the spatial area occupied by the armadillo? The answer is one of scale. On a statewide basis, the occupied area has remained fairly stable for the past thirty years. But fluctuations take place on the local or county level when animals congregate near water sources in dry spells or spread out in wetter periods. With well-filled creeks and stock ponds, armadillos may be widely distributed in a county although numbers may not be large. Wildlife experts have commented on this response to moisture at the local level many times in the last several decades. A pattern of periodic advances and retreats is most apparent in West Texas and where water shortages are most frequent.

Western and northwestern Texas, approximately beyond a line from Wichita Falls to Del Rio, is a zone of marginal habitat for the nine-banded armadillo. The distribution and densities of animals vary greatly in this marginal zone. In riparian areas, along the upper Colorado and Concho rivers for example, one armadillo per 10 acres is not uncommon. But on the drier divides animal density may decrease to one animal per 100 acres, and as one drives toward New Mexico or into the High Plains, armadillos are encountered only rarely. Northward and westward, therefore, the marginal zone becomes a "sterile" region where individuals may wander occasionally, but where average temperature and moisture regimes preclude permanent populations. We can safely say that any prolonged western movement into the Trans-Pecos and Panhandle of Texas, into New Mexico, and into western Oklahoma is most unlikely.[41]

Establishing the armadillo's northern limit in the United States is much more difficult. This adaptable mammal has scotched earlier predictions that it would not survive harsher winters in north-central Texas by crossing the Red River into Oklahoma and Arkansas, where it flourishes.

One biologist has explained away this phenomenon by

suggesting that the "winter cold barrier" may have retreated northward ahead of the armadillo, thereby permitting animals to inhabit areas where many people believed they could not survive.[42] It is probable that the armadillo is now approaching this heralded "cold threshold" in southern Kansas and Missouri. Individuals occasionally turn up in both states, but so far they have not been able to survive on a permanent basis, even after so-called "mild" winters. The situation is further complicated in that some armadillos in central parts may be more affected by cold weather than others in the north. During the late 1970s, unusually cold winters in the lower Midwest and Deep South reportedly had little effect on armadillos in northern Oklahoma and central Arkansas. However, a mortality increase that was attributed to prolonged cold spells was noted in southern Arkansas, central Mississippi, and north-central Texas. This anomaly may be due to disparate interest in this mammal in such places.

Nevertheless, current conditions suggest that northern Mississippi and Alabama are places "waiting" to be occupied by armadillos. The same may be said for southwestern Tennessee and the coastal plain of Georgia and South Carolina. In eastern Tennessee, northern Georgia and northwestern South Carolina, the Appalachian uplands may be a barrier to range extension. Winters are generally colder in the Blue Ridge Mountains.

So far we have dealt only with range extension and environmental barriers as they relate to the "core area" for armadillos in the south-central and southeastern United States. A more speculative issue is whether armadillos could flourish in natural or human-altered landscapes in the Southwest. Could armadillos survive on golf courses in Phoenix or Palm Springs, or in the irrigated croplands or well-watered subdivisions in California's lower Central Valley? The answer is probably yes. And the same may be said about Hawaii or Puerto Rico, where there is no temperature or moisture barrier to prevent them from thriving. We know from past experience in Florida, Mississippi, and Alabama that accidental or intentional release of one gravid armadillo, or a pair, is sufficient to start a resident population. In spite of measures by wildlife agencies in western states that prohibit the introduction of new mammals, especially alien species, the current infatuation with the nine-banded armadillo and the increasing popularity of armadillo racing could result in new colonization. It is a situation that needs vigilance. Meanwhile, in the Southeast, through a combination of natural spread and human-induced transportation and releases, the armadillo is expanding its range and exceeds the limits of distribution that experts set for it in the early 1970s.

3. Human Use of the Armadillo

The armadillo is considered a legitimate game animal in South Texas and the southern states, and there are few restrictions on hunting it. Fifty years ago many people treated armadillos as vermin, and, especially in rural areas, some still do. For many years, entrepreneurs sold armadillo shells as decorative baskets and wall ornaments. A sizable trade in these oddities included live armadillos sold as pets. That practice has ended, but today "armadillo races" are frequently featured at local fairs, armadillo meat is a common item in chili recipes and cook-offs, and barbecued armadillo is said by gourmands to taste like pork, chicken, or even sea turtle. It is cooked for game dinners and is sold in specialty restaurants in some larger Texas cities.

Additionally, the armadillo has been the subject of intensive scientific, particularly medical research in genetics and reproductive physiology, for approximately eighty years. Quite recently, scientists successfully infected nine-banded armadillos with leprosy, and have discovered a leprosy-like disease that occurs naturally in wild armadillos in at least three states. Lepromin, a diagnostic reagent used for determining degrees of human resistance to leprosy, is now derived from the tissues of armadillos infected with leprosy bacillus in the laboratory and in the wild. Centers for disease research and control are, therefore, extremely interested in using armadillos for experiments to develop a vaccine against leprosy.

THE APELT ARMADILLO COMPANY

Baskets, lampshades, wall hangings, and other ornaments fashioned from the shells of armadillos first appeared in Central Texas about the turn of the present century. German-born immigrant Charles Apelt, farmer, basket maker, and founder of the Apelt Armadillo Company near Comfort, Texas, is credited with inventing the "shell basket," and his enterprise has been included in the local folklore of the Hill Country.[1] Other firms were believed to be "equally active" before World War I;[2] but Apelt's "armadillo farm" seems to have dominated the business and outlasted all competition, continuing operations until about 1971. Details about the Apelt Armadillo Company can be pieced together from partial records and from persons familiar with its operations; other dealers sold baskets in Boerne, near Comfort, and hawked them along the border, probably importing the animal-skin containers from Mexico. These trading practices are now forgotten, but they offered similar products and presumably operated along lines similar to Apelt's.

Details about the curio trade in armadillo shells remain sketchy. According to newspaper accounts dating back to the 1920s, Charles Apelt (1862–1944), sometimes written Appelt, came from Germany in about 1887 to visit relatives on a farm in Kerr County near Comfort. During his stay, Charles' uncle was reportedly killed when his wagon overturned. Although their nephew had no previous farming experience, his aunt, Mrs. Reinhold Kutzer, assisted him to remain and work on the 115-acre farm.[3]

Several years later, as Charles was working on the farm, he caught sight of his first "moving rock"—the armadillo. According to family recollections, Apelt heaved a stone or two at the strange animal, hit it on the head, and killed it. Keeping the skins of "varmints" for sale or barter was a widespread custom and included this odd-looking creature. Apelt was to recall that after he skinned his first armadillo, he forgot about it and went on with his chores. When he finally returned to tack the skin to the shed door, he discovered that his trophy had curled up in the sun and resembled a crude container. As he looked at his first armadillo shell, so the story goes, Charles realized what a fine basket it would make. Back in Germany, Apelt and his family had worked as basket makers, fashioning containers and furniture from willow and rushes. Almost by instinct, therefore, Charles believed that this armadillo would become an interesting basket too; it was probably much easier to make up than the tiresome process of weaving willow branches and other vegetation that he had practiced as a boy. From that day on, he devoted more and more of his attention and energy to studying this unusual but increasingly abundant native mammal. He established a novel home industry to flourish as the Armadillo Farm and Basket Factory, also named the Apelt Armadillo Company.[4]

It is not entirely correct to refer to the Apelt operation as a "farm." Armadillos were confined and even raised on the premises for sale to zoos, to scientists for research, and to people as pets. Charles' son Kurt recalled that after 1900 researchers would come to Comfort and kill and dissect animals in the pens. However, much of Charles Apelt's operation involved hunting wild armadillos near Comfort and in the surrounding Hill Country in order to make baskets from their shells and to pen others for live shipment.

Armadillo Hunters

Apelt's business in shell baskets grew rapidly. County tax records and other information suggest that he began operations in 1898, when his name appeared as "Carl Apelt and Co." on Kerr County records.[5] Family and friends back in Germany admired these basket curios from Texas, and encouraged him to send more. Local outlets grew promising too, so that Charles began to hire hunters to scour the creek banks and limestone uplands around Comfort and Kerrville in search of armadillos, which were becoming more common. In the 1920s, at the height of the firm's success, Apelt employed more than fifty men to capture animals and prepare shells. Armed with clubs and accompanied by tracking dogs, these professional hunters were directed by a retired Army officer known as "the Colonel." Operating from his base at Ingram, northwest of Kerrville, the Colonel and his "armadillo army" made a living hunting armadillos. A popular article about basket making which appeared in *Farm and Ranch* in 1928 suggested that for 75 cents per dressed shell, hunters could make a useful profit.[6]

Working for the most part in the evening and at night, the men sent their dogs on the trail of rooting armadillos. They placed muzzles on the dogs to prevent them from biting into and thereby damaging an armadillo's shell, so that on tracking down the scattering animals they would harass and corner them until hunters could club the creatures on the back of the skull and kill them. As many armadillos reportedly "froze" when blinded by the light from a hunter's lantern, hitting them on the head was simple. Some animals would dig furiously to escape, so that the men had to jerk the hind legs off the ground in order to loosen the tenacious grip of powerful claws that quickly enabled the animal to submerge itself. In seizing a tail that might be seen to be protruding from a burrow, it was important to make sure it belonged to one of these "armored battleships," and not to a rattlesnake. Apelt reported that several hunters had been mortally bitten by snakes after mistaking one for an armadillo's tail, or when reaching into darkened cavities or dens where the mammals might hide.[7] Once secured and dispatched, the carcass was skinned and cleaned in the field, the flesh being scooped out of the shell with a device designed especially for that purpose.

The demand for armadillo shells grew, slackening temporarily during World War I, although one source suggested that people stationed at military bases around San Antonio helped to broaden the popularity of armadillo baskets. It became known that Apelt would pay cash for good shells.[8] Farmers wishing to supplement incomes or school-aged youths after pocket change found hunting armadillos a good way to pick up extra money. Animals carried to the farm by these part-time hunters fetched about 25 cents each. Apparently knowledge of this unusual source of cash persisted after the demand for armadillos had declined. One journalist who interviewed Kurt Apelt in 1967 was given the story about the armadillo farm on condition that readers should be instructed not to bring armadillos to Comfort. Kurt complained that "every time they put something in the papers about our place, people start hauling armadillos in here to sell . . . bringing them in by the truckload."[9]

Basket Makers

Hunters brought in armadillo shells to the Apelt farm to be made up into baskets, lampshades, wall ornaments, and other oddments. Charles Apelt treated the shells with a "secret formula" to make them insect-proof and to prevent deterioration. He also had a crew of men and women who cleaned, shaped, polished, and lined the shell baskets with silk and satin.

Many employees worked on the dried shells in nearby Hill Country communities, where a good basket maker could turn out approximately one hundred baskets a week. Noah and Charles Knox of Ingram in Kerr County subcontracted with Apelt as basket makers. Mr. Shirley from Pipe Creek in Bandera County and Ira Gassoway from Utopia in Uvalde County also worked regularly for the factory. Some of the best work was done by the Albert Evans family of Priddy in Mills County. Fritz Burrow of Comfort reportedly made a few baskets, too; and other locals sewed colored basket linings made from lightweight cloths. For the most part, however, it seems that the citizens of Comfort regarded the armadillo basket operation as a strange business.

After the shell of the armadillo was cleaned, its tail was looped underneath and attached to the head to form the handle for the basket. It was then left to dry for several days in the sun. Shells for lamps, wall hangings, and similar devices were shaped in the same way, then "scientifically treated" so that, as an Apelt brochure proclaimed, they carried a guarantee to be greaseless, insect-proof, and completely sanitary.[10]

Apelt at one time offered a plain, untrimmed basket in natural colors for as little as $2.50. More expensive ones were made with variously colored silk linings, or with bows and beads, according to a customer's taste, and sold for as much as $15.00 each. Cloth linings were sewed onto the shell, not glued; and, if desired, the shell or its handle could be painted to match the color of the lining.

For $25.00 Apelt sold hand-wrought iron floor and table lamps topped by armadillo shell lampshades with hand-made bead fringes. There was a wide variety of color combinations and shapes to choose from, and one of Apelt's lamp masterpieces was a large chandelier made up from five shells. Additionally, as a conversation piece, for $19.50 a customer could purchase an "armadillo completa," namely, a stuffed animal mounted in "such a lifelike way as to confuse the observer."[11]

The Basket Trade

From the late 1890s until his death in 1944, Apelt built up an international business in armadillo artifacts. At first, his retail outlets were limited to nearby communities and to towns along the Mexican border. Scientist John K. Strecker came across armadillo baskets in San Antonio in 1896 and was told that most of the animals had been killed in Cameron and Hidalgo counties in the lower Rio Grande Valley.[12] It appears that Apelt had competitors.

In 1913, biologist Henry H. Newman reported that a dealer—it may have been Apelt—shipped over 40,000 baskets in a six-year period before World War I; and at least two other firms were equally active. Another source indicated that a game dealer from Laredo purchased armadillo shells every year in Goliad County to be made into baskets. The same source reported that "carloads" of shells were sold from Colorado County, especially before 1930. Who purchased them is not known.[13]

Apelt shipped his baskets and other armadillo shell products from his Comfort facility to all parts of the world. His brother in Muhlberg, Germany, acted as an exclusive agent for Western Europe, and an early catalogue printed in German described the Apelt baskets in detail. In the early 1920s, when his crew was most active, trade was very brisk and included shipments to New Zealand and Australia. During that decade a number of reporters and writers for popular journals stressed the novelty of Apelt's factory, which also had a sideline in starfish lamps, Aztec pottery, coconut baskets, and rattlesnake skins.

Apelt and his wife, Martha (1870–1947), operated a shop next to the farm and ran a mail-order business. The Buckhorn Saloon in San Antonio and a curio dealer in Capetown, South Africa, proved to be among their largest outlets. Success had been achieved, according to Apelt's promotional brochure, because of the uniqueness of his product, experimentation to produce high quality and attractive baskets, and management of healthy animals for trading as pets. Apelt promoted the enterprise through "scientific advertising" and guaranteed that customers would be satisfied with their purchases.[14]

During the half-century that Apelt operated his armadillo farm, he shipped out hundreds of thousands of baskets, lamps, and other items. His daughter-in-law, Kathryn Apelt (later Mrs. Kathryn Jorns) recalled selling more than twenty thousand armadillos and armadillo products in a single year.[15] The extent of the demand was a principal factor in a decision to keep and raise armadillos in captivity so that live animals could be furnished to zoos and to medical institutions.

Captive Armadillos

After World War I, Apelt noted a decline in the number of wild armadillos, which he attributed to forest fires in the Hill Country, not to overhunting. These apparent fluctuations in population influenced his decision to try to breed armadillos in captivity. Several authorities have questioned whether Apelt was ever successful in breeding and raising a steady supply of armadillos, or merely held pregnant females in captivity until they produced their four offspring.[16]

There are arguments to suggest that Apelt was able to breed animals in captivity. During the several decades that he was in the armadillo business, hundreds of tourists and scientists were shown live armadillos on the premises all year round. A medical researcher recalled that before 1913 Apelt was able to furnish him with large numbers of armadillos on a regular basis, although some were doubtless specimens captured in the wild.

In order to keep armadillos, Apelt constructed an elaborate network of pens complete with artificial burrows and shelters. A leaflet, *A Mother Armadillo with Four Young*, was included with shipments of live animals, and provided information about care and feeding schedules that Apelt had developed from years of experience.

The enclosures that Apelt set up included burrows and tunnels made from concrete. Several less elaborate pens were built with fences that were sunk several feet into the ground in order to prevent captives from digging out. During winter months, Apelt kept animals in small sheds and supplied liberal amounts of hay for insulation. During the day and especially in bad weather, animals would burrow into the hay or disappear into the underground runways and remain there as long as a cold spell lasted, coming out only for food.

Apelt fed his captive armadillos milk, eggs, greens, raw

meat, and table scraps, a diet that he modified to include canned dog food. Armadillos, which are essentially insectivorous in the wild, apparently adjusted successfully to this varied diet in captivity. Zoo-held armadillos, including the genus *Dasypus*, consume horsemeat and Purina Mink Developer Chow, to which is added a blend of hard-boiled eggs, honey, molasses, and liquid multivitamins. Serious blood loss from minor injuries and lacerations has been stopped by providing a source of Vitamin K.[17]

Armadillos reproduce when about two years old, and a ratio of one male to ten females was kept on the Apelt farm for "breeding stock." After the birth of the litter, usually in March or April, the male was removed from the pen.

Apelt shipped live armadillos from Comfort via the Southern Pacific Railroad. Later, as air transportation became more common and less expensive, he sent animals by air express from San Antonio. Apelt supplied small lots or pairs of armadillos to zoos and circuses throughout the country. According to Kathryn Apelt Jorns, one pair that he shipped to Florida escaped or was released, and game authorities contacted Charles about possible ways of eradicating armadillo numbers that they feared would pose a threat to agriculture.

Hunters came from all parts of the country to hunt white-tailed deer in the Hill Country and frequently visited the Comfort armadillo farm. As a practical joke, many of them sent live armadillos to friends. Recipients of such novel pets, which reportedly would respond to gentle handling by becoming "tame and obedient," would have needed to be "night owls," as armadillos are commonly nocturnal in captivity. New owners were instructed to feed their charges a mixture of raw eggs and meat, tender grass or alfalfa, and "canned PARD dog food," and set up a cage with a net wire sunk 12–18 inches in the ground in order to stop them from escaping.[18] Some of these armored curiosities doubtless burrowed or climbed quickly to freedom. Most probably, people released them once the novelty of such unsolicited gifts wore thin and the noise of nighttime activities made them intolerable.

Farm Operations after Apelt

Kathryn Apelt, Charles Apelt's daughter-in-law, came from Kentucky, where there are no armadillos. She saw her first armadillo in a short film about Apelt's farm, *Strange Occupations*, made by Paramount Pictures. A short time later, Kathryn met and married Kurt, Charles' third son (1899–1972). Kathryn was to take an active part in the armadillo enterprise, although her husband had inherited very little of his father's enthusiasm for the creatures.

After Charles Apelt died, his wife, Martha, took over the business until her own death. Martha had an affection for the armadillos on the farm, and she made it a firm rule that only "wild" armadillos were to be used for baskets.[19] Her daughter, Ruth, the fourth Apelt child, assumed control of the business in 1947 and then moved the operation, including the shop's inventory, to Salado in Bell County, Texas, about 100 miles northeast of Comfort. The venture under Ruth Apelt (whose married name was Dowdy) sold live armadillos from $5–9 a pair and used hunters with dogs to catch animals by stunning them with a blow across the exposed upper body, thereby keeping their shells intact. The new farm did not prosper, however. It closed down when armadillo hunters and their hounds proved hard to attract in spite of the sizable demand for baskets. According to Kathryn Apelt, several employees returned to Comfort and encouraged her to reopen the Comfort armadillo farm. Kathryn agreed to do this in 1951.[20]

At the time, she had no live armadillos and only a small supply of baskets and other curios, but with the help of some long-time friends and basket makers, Kathryn soon expanded commercial operations. Trade in live armadillos increased as well, and as business picked up, numbers were sent regularly to medical schools and university research centers. Rice University in Houston and Dartmouth College in Hanover, New Hampshire, were among the most regular customers. Live armadillos were also sent abroad, to medical institutions in Belgium and Germany. One animal was sent to a school for the blind in Michigan, but Kathryn was reluctant to send the animals to public schools, where she believed that many of them would die because of improper care and handling. She claims that "thousands of armadillos were sold as pets" over the years, and others were sent to zoos "in every state in the Union." On occasion, animals were sent to an outlet in nearby New Braunfels for resale to tourists and to research facilities.

According to Kathryn Apelt Jorns, there were "worlds of armadillos from Comfort to Halletsville; we never had any trouble getting them." She recalls that on one occasion an order was placed for 30 pregnant females. However, only 23 pregnant animals were among the 150 or so animals the hunters captured.

The Apelt Armadillo Company finally closed in 1971. During more than seventy years, tens of thousands of armadillo baskets, other decorative items, and live animals were sold from the farm shop, and through mail order. Other dealers, such as W. A. "Snake King" King of Brownsville and J. W. Johnson of Laredo, who sold various mammals and birds, also carried armadillos and armadillo products.[21]

THE SAN ANGELO CONNECTION

In the early 1970s, after the Apelt Armadillo Company closed, medical schools and other research facilities were temporarily without a source of armadillos. They turned to Sam Lewis, entrepreneur from San Angelo, Texas, inventor of the jalapeño lollipop and promoter of armadillo races.[22]

Lewis' connections with medical schools are not particularly substantial. He has two regular customers, the University of Hawaii and a medical school in the United Kingdom.

Lewis sends usually two to ten animals to client universities five to seven times per year. The University of Hawaii, which uses armadillos for leprosy research, receives only male armadillos. According to Lewis, this is a precautionary measure to eliminate the risk of introducing armadillos which might escape and breed in an island ecosystem, which is already loaded with alien mammals and birds. The British medical facility, on the other hand, requires only female armadillos for studies in reproductive physiology. Lewis has sold armadillos to zoos in the United States and abroad on an irregular basis. In 1980 he supplied four armadillos, euphemistically called "Texas pandas," to the National Zoo in Peking, China, at the request of an employee of a Houston-based oil company.[23]

Lewis ships armadillos by air freight from Dallas or Houston to destinations more than one day's drive from San Angelo. The animals are placed in plywood crates, a maximum of six armadillos per container. Steps are taken to minimize stress, but losses do occur. An 80 percent survival rate per international shipment is considered good.

Lewis and his associates capture armadillos from "all over" Texas, but most animals come from the Hill Country of the Edwards Plateau. Frequently, San Angelo residents call Sam when they find a "gravedigger" rooting in their lawns and gardens.

Lewis' armadillos are held in cages 12 feet long, 4 feet wide, and 2 feet high. The height of the cage was determined after it was discovered that armadillos are adept climbers. The 2-foot-high walls allow most armadillos to stand at full height, but remain low enough to prevent them from climbing and risking injury from a fall. The caged armadillos are provided with small "nesting boxes" made of plywood and packed with shredded newspaper for nesting and insulation. Lewis has used hay and straw, but he believes that his armadillos develop respiratory problems more easily when such plant material is used as bedding. No additional insulation is given during winter, except that a sheet of clear plastic covers each cage to keep rain and dampness out.

Newly captured armadillos are fed soft scrambled eggs to which a small amount of bacon grease is added. Later, as a wild animal becomes more accustomed to confinement, it is fed commercially prepared dog food "burgers," chopped chicken livers, and an occasional raw egg. Lewis has noted that an armadillo will sometimes ignore eggs for a while. Then, when it decides to eat one, the armadillo will break it open by pushing the shell against the frame of the cage.

In the wild, armadillos ingest soil when rooting for grubs and insects. Apparently this habit is not accidental, as Lewis insists that his armadillos must have access to dirt in order to avoid gastro-intestinal problems. So animals in transit and those held in cages with wood or metal floors have soil added to their food at the rate of one or two cups per eight pounds of food. Lewis has also experimented with a layer of sand covering the bottom of the cage, but he found that armadillos kicked the sand away to get at the soil below.

Lewis makes no special effort to enable armadillos to reproduce in captivity. However, one wild female gave birth to a healthy litter in captivity in late January 1979. The same female mated with a captive male in the late summer of 1979 and again bore four young in January 1980. Lewis keeps male and female armadillos together throughout the year, but mating has not occurred on a regular basis.

PREDATORY ARMADILLOS

In May 1929, L. C. Whitehead, who headed a federal rodent control operation from San Antonio, alerted his superiors in the Bureau of Biological Survey, Washington, D.C., that farmers in Grimes, Jasper, and Kendall counties were complaining about armadillos digging up and doing "considerable damage to sprouting green crops." Whitehead asked whether he should poison the offending enemies. Stanley P. Young, who was in charge of economic investigations of animal food habits with the Biological Survey, was surprised. "This is the first time the Bureau has been advised that armadillos are injurious to vegetation," he replied, advising Whitehead to move slowly because of the animal's reported value in consuming insects.[24]

Whitehead continued to press for control. In 1930, he noted a growing demand to eradicate this increasingly numerous mammal because reports had come in about armadillos consuming alfalfa and being "decidedly injurious in destroying eggs of ground-nesting birds and in rooting up corn crops." Additionally, several breaks in levees along the Trinity River were blamed on burrowing armadillos. Accordingly, Whitehead recommended that strychnine be used to poison offending animals. However, he admitted that "conservationists" would probably object to this method of control, so he withheld criticism of the animal from the final draft of his annual report on operations against such vermin as gophers, rats, jackrabbits, and prairie dogs.[25]

An increasing number of questions about the animal's food preferences, plus complaints about damage to crops and wild turkey and quail nests, continued to descend on Washington, D.C. Cedric Landon, Whitehead's coworker, who specialized in trapping and poisoning predatory wolves, coyotes, bobcats, and cougars in Texas, added his voice to the growing controversy about food habits of the armadillo. Landon notified Young about "the number of requests for the control of these animals," which some hunters accused of feeding on game bird eggs, while some farmers praised them for consuming pestiferous insects.[26]

Matters came to a head in 1933. Initial laboratory tests at the federal research station in Denver suggested that armadillos were useful as insect destroyers; however, field trials were called for. Accordingly, William L. McAtee, a government biologist who investigated the food habits of mammals and birds, and to whom the matter was referred, contacted William J. Tucker, first Executive Secretary for the Texas

Game, Fish and Oyster Commission, about finding a suitable place for studying the armadillo's diet. Tucker responded to McAtee's letter, which included a comment about the "alleged destruction of quail and other birds," by naming Pearsall in Frio County as a good locality for pioneering research. He also included in his letter certain favorable comments about armadillos.[27]

Texas game warden Frank Smith argued that quail and armadillos did not appear to conflict—the birds tended to keep to upland areas and the mammals to river valleys—at least around Pearsall. Interestingly, Smith did not believe that armadillos affected nesting bobwhites. His comment, which Tucker passed on verbatim to the food habits research group, was, "I will do all I can [to assist the study] for I want to see my little friend the armadillo's skirts cleared of this crime that is being heaped on his back by a lot of circumstantial evidence and the talk of a lot of town dudes who do not know an armadillo from a dry-land terrapin."[28]

After obtaining Tucker's support, Biological Survey officials dispatched biologist Edward R. Kalmbach, who headed up the laboratory on food habits in Denver, Colorado, to supervise field work on armadillo diets. Six weeks of study included a visit with people in the Ingram and Kerrville area (possibly Apelt's basket makers), who agreed to furnish armadillo stomachs for analysis. However, field tests in two sites near Cleveland and Shepard in the south-central post oak belt proved inconclusive about the mammal's taste for bird eggs. Foraging armadillos were not much interested in quail nests, nor in the "dummy" nests that researchers had fashioned to resemble real ones. Kalmbach could not persuade a wild armadillo to break open a chicken egg that he placed repeatedly in its path. Captive animals cracked a few eggs more by accident than design before they climbed out of their cages and escaped.[29]

With substantial assistance from Valgene Lehmann, a biology graduate student who subsequently became an authority on prairie chickens and bobwhite quail, Kalmbach made up two hundred "dummy" nests in late May and June 1933. These nests were supplied with chicken eggs and monitored near Brenham, Lehmann's home base, and Cleveland. Skunks, ringtailed cats, and crows proved to be the chief egg thieves. Armadillos did not figure among the seven categories of egg filchers and nest destroyers that included cattle and roadrunners.[30]

Kalmbach's initial survey, therefore, exonerated armadillos from the charge of being harmful to nesting quail, and, despite accusations from local farmers that armadillos destroyed corn and muskmelon and watermelon patches, the biologist judged that other animals were the primary culprits in bird and crop destruction. Without canine or incisor teeth it was difficult, if not impossible, for the edentates to gnaw into melons, although they would opportunistically feed on broken ones. Kalmbach did admit, however, that armadillos damaged peanuts, and he confirmed local lore that armadillos could cross creeks by simply walking across under the water. After repeatedly flinging an armadillo into a large pond he also saw it swim dog-like to the shore, and after killing and dissecting it, Kalmbach noted that its intestines had become inflated, providing buoyancy.[31]

Whitehead included Kalmbach's initial experiments in his 1933 annual summary of "rodent" work in Texas, but received better corroboration about the animal's alleged habit of preying on eggs from field work the following year, which did find that some armadillos took quail eggs, although not in large quantities. After a decade of interest and research into Texas armadillos, Kalmbach published his findings with the Texas Game, Fish and Oyster Commission. Ninety-three percent of an armadillo's food consisted of animal materials. Insects comprised most of it (78 percent), while amphibians and reptiles totaled merely 1.2 percent. The remainder consisted of spiders, millipedes, earthworms, slugs, etc. Bird eggs were present in only 5 of 281 stomachs. The armadillo was not considered a menace to ground nesting birds, and on balance, it was judged to be much more beneficial than harmful.[32]

Over the last twenty years the U.S. Fish and Wildlife Service's Branch of Predator and Rodent Control has been more concerned about armadillos in suburban places. Nursery owners and gardeners have little affection for these nocturnal visitors, which root among flowerbeds, damage shrubs and lawns, and feed on golf courses and football and baseball fields. A leaflet from the Division of Wildlife Services in Gainesville, Florida, where armadillos are widespread, encouraged hunters to shoot armadillos and dress them for meat. In metropolitan areas, capture by stalking with a "long-handled fishing net" was preferred to poisoning or gassing them in their dens, as such operations were hazardous to other animals. Fencing, although more costly, was also recommended to keep armadillos out of vulnerable crops and sensitive areas; however, problems from armadillo activities—especially in summer—continued to crop up.[33]

Newsworthy "invasions" or "occupations" in the Dallas region were reported in the mid-1950s, when Wills Point in Van Zandt County was overrun by hungry armadillos. These mobile animals made friends with local dogs and became enemies of all the gardeners. One resident grumbled about their fondness for "caladium bulbs, ivy and other store-boughten goodies" in her yard. Neighborhood dogs had reportedly come to "some kind of non-aggression pact with the armadillos."[34]

In the early 1960s it was the turn of Eustace in Henderson County to be the "Texas town most overrun by armadillos." Armadillos denned under homes and even scuttled into living rooms through open doors. Other places, including Shreveport, Louisiana, and Venice, Florida, have found armadillos a nuisance too, and local agricultural agents and county officials usually take care of such outbreaks.[35]

Complaints about damage in Texas have tended to center

on metropolitan areas with burgeoning suburban developments. The highest number of complaints from 1975 to 1979 came from Austin (294) and Houston (199), as construction sliced into suitable habitat. There appears to be a correlation between the onset of breeding in July and complaints about garden damage, when females and their young root most intensively for food and discover well-watered lawns and recreational areas as optimal feeding stations.[36] Richardson, in the Dallas–Fort Worth metroplex, had its problems in September 1982, when some yards looked as if "miniature hogs" had passed through them. Organizers of the World Armadillo Olympics in Nahunta, Georgia, came up with one novel solution—catch as many animals as possible, race them, and then exterminate them to free the southern Georgia farm belt from such rooting pests. The venture fell through in the spring of 1982, because a hard winter decimated the estimated twenty thousand armadillos in Brantley County and the festival's founders had to cancel the event.[37]

THE ARMADILLO AS FOOD

The custom of eating armadillos has been common in rural areas for as long as the animal has been in Texas. During hard times, particularly during the Great Depression in the 1930s, the armadillo earned the title "poor man's pig" for its pork-like taste. It was a staple food in rural Texas. J. Frank Dobie commented in 1961 that a good part of the country "was becoming well-stocked with armadillo meat for the next Depression. During the last one, armadillos got the name of 'Hoover hogs' in East Texas" In 1982, a newspaperman from Nacogdoches speculated that Democrats would be calling them "Ronnie's rooters" if the economy did not improve. People, it seems, will make do with armadillo meat when they have to.[38]

In his pioneering 1905 report, Vernon Bailey noted that armadillos were very common in the lower Rio Grande Valley around Brownsville and were "much sought after for eating purposes." Almost forty years later, federal scientist Edward R. Kalmbach reported that armadillos were commonly eaten by both black and white residents in many parts of Texas, and also by Mexicans and Indians south of the border. He also claimed that about 300 armadillos were killed and eaten on one ranch east of Cuero in DeWitt County in south-central Texas during January and February 1940.[39]

Residents in South Texas reportedly hunted armadillos regularly and considered them "legitimate and desirable game, almost on par with quail." Seven game wardens, responding to a 1938–1939 survey that was part of an effort to ascertain the status of important game mammals and birds, reported that armadillos were hunted regularly for food, especially in South and Southeast Texas. Some persons declared that armadillo meat was as finely flavored as pork or even sea turtle and advocated experiments in canning it. H. A. Clapp, a canning specialist for Texas A&M, judged that armadillo meat was equal in quality to anything that he had eaten, and he encouraged others to make use of this fine food. Under his direction, more than two thousand cans of armadillo meat were put up in the late 1920s. In 1958, two grocery stores in Houston offered dressed armadillos ready for cooking for $1.50 each, and reportedly sold forty to fifty per week.[40] Armadillos have not been universally accepted as a delicacy, however. Kalmbach noted that farmers in Mason County "were reported boiling and chopping up the meat of armadillos as food for poultry and dogs." In East Texas a man used armadillos for hog feed; and in Louisiana, residents who "considered raccoon and possum legitimate game, expressed revulsion at the idea of eating an armadillo." Recently, however, it has been learned that in the area around Baton Rouge and New Orleans, armadillos are now a common food item. In Arkansas, "where armadillos are well established, they are used for human consumption

. . . barbecued armadillo is considered tasty dining fare by many."[41]

When Kathryn Apelt managed the Apelt Armadillo Company, she was approached by a man from New York who asked her to provide canned armadillo meat for his restaurant. She declined because she believed that it was not worth the work and expense; however, she reported that a buyer from San Antonio took armadillo meat from the old Apelt farm to wild game banquets around the country.[42]

Armadillo meat is a curiosity for many people. At a 1969 wild game dinner in Centerville, Leon County, baked armadillo proved more popular than other gourmet dishes such as raccoon and collard greens, opossum with yams, and pot roast of beaver. There were people, however, who found the whole idea of eating armadillo too unsavory. After seeing such slogans as "Try Armadillo on the Half Shell," under the banner of the Armadillo Breeders Association based in Dallas, one East Texas resident found it all too boorish and brutal. Columnist Frank X. Tolbert, who noted these details, remained unsympathetic, reporting that an armadillo ranch in Blanco County was trying to upgrade armadillos "for better steaks and roasts." Today, game dinners to raise funds for local charities, building projects, and other municipal events commonly place barbecued armadillo on the menu with venison, turkey, quail, and squirrel.[43]

The armadillo's reputation as a substitute for pork has earned it a place in Texas folklore. In a collection of folk tales, "Big Thicket Balladry," it was said that "when pork is scarce, some families fill their smokehouses with armadillos, skinned and smoked over hickory fires." There are risks in consuming armadillos though. Another folk tale, "The Mystery of the Five Graves," is the story of a family named Larkin, early settlers in the Eagle Pass area, who one evening cooked and ate an armadillo that had been killed by a dog. The father and his sons were "poisoned" by the contaminated meat and died.[44] Along this same line, young boys in

South Texas who hunt armadillos for food are taught to make a head shot lest the meat become tainted.

In Texas, the armadillo was more or less legitimized as a game food by the Texas Parks and Wildlife Department, which published a number of recipes for armadillo in its monthly periodical over the past forty years. One recent article suggested, however, that many people shy away from eating armadillo meat because of the animal's unpleasant odor. Nevertheless, barbecued armadillo and armadillo-based chili recipes are accepted and popular. One of the simplest and best known of them belonged to the late Hondo Crouch, who for years presided as the mayor of Luckenbach. His recipe called for "one medium armadillo, other stuff, save the shell, serves four." It was noted that Hondo entered a mixture of venison and armadillo meat as "pure armadillo chili" in the World's Chili Cook-Off in Terlingua in 1969, when a state representative proposed the armadillo as the "Official Beast of the City of Terlingua," famed for its chili cook-off festivals. Crouch also recommended a diet of armadillo for any person working to lose weight. "You eat nothing but armadillo for a month," he said, "and you have to run down and catch all the armadillos you eat—really takes the weight off!"[45]

Similar expressions come from eastern parts of the animal's contemporary range, namely Florida. Wildlife experts have supplied instructions about dressing armadillos and suggested attractive recipes. One must cut the belly skin near the shell all the way around to pull the carcass away from it. Then one cuts off the feet and head, shears through the breast and pelvic bones, and removes all innards, including fat and sweat glands. After washing, the carcass is then ready to cook, and may be baked, barbecued, or fried, and stuffed with sweet potatoes.[46]

In Mexico, residents consume the meat and use armadillo oil as a treatment for rheumatism. The oil is also employed among the Mexican-American population in Texas for softening and preserving leather.

As noted in the following section on armadillos in medical research, some health experts recently have expressed concerns about the safety of handling and eating armadillos, due to the discovery of leprosy in wild armadillos. The greatest risk would reportedly come from handling live animals or raw meat or tissue. A possible pathway linking armadillos to human leprosy, which is not highly communicable, would be in frequent contact with animals over a number of years and suffering cuts and abrasions when catching or cleaning them. (See pp. 76–77.)

ARMADILLOS IN MEDICAL RESEARCH

Since early in this century, the nine-banded armadillo has been the subject of medical and scientific research in such fields as cytology, reproductive physiology, and genetics. In 1909–1911, University of Texas zoologists Henry H. Newman and J. Thomas Patterson published three papers on heredity and embryology in the nine-banded armadillo. In pioneering research on the "limits of hereditary control," Newman and Patterson concluded that variation in the number and shape of bands over the thoraco-lumbar region, the body's so-called "armor shield" and "a protective structure of high efficiency in an otherwise defenseless animal," was governed by chance. In these early publications, the Austin-based scientists referred to "an extensive curio industry, making a specialty of baskets shaped from the shells of armadillos," and they scrutinized 1,768 individual animals for band abnormalities from "a large stock of basket-shells in the hands of various dealers."[47]

Newman and Patterson also demonstrated the existence of specific polyembryony: that all sets of embryos were the product of the division of a single fertilized egg. Subsequent researchers have built on such studies. Some people have become interested in the ability of the female "pocket battle-ship" to delay the development of the embryo for up to twenty months, making the armadillo's gestation period almost as long as an elephant's![48] Other researchers have concentrated on the scientific and especially the potential medical value of having identical quadruplet mammals to work with. Siblings are of the same sex and genetically identical; however, individuals may show variations in heart or spleen size, or differences in acids and other body chemicals—differences that are greater than one might expect. Unfortunately, it has proved extremely difficult to establish a program of sustained breeding in captivity so that researchers can easily produce and test sets of animals under controlled conditions.[49]

Frank Weaker, professor of anatomy at the University of Texas Health Science Center in San Antonio, has tried to get armadillos to breed in captivity. Weaker usually captured his own animals, but occasionally purchased them from a commercial supply house. One winter Weaker needed animals, so he ordered them from a dealer in Florida. The supplier told him that the shipment would be delayed for several weeks—until the hard weather in Texas improved, as his stock came from the Texas Hill Country. It seems that animal supply houses throughout the South still rely on part-time hunters to supply armadillos, which are then shipped to other parts of the country. Texas remains a major source region for captive stock.[50]

An important use of armadillos in medical research is in studies of leprosy. Leprosy, or Hansen's Disease (HD) as it is officially called, is an infection whose cause was first discovered by Norwegian scientist Gerhard A. Hansen in 1873. The tiny bacilli (rod-shaped bacteria) of *Mycobacterium leprae* affect the skin, peripheral nerves, and sometimes the respiratory tract, eye, muscles, and reproductive organs. People dread leprosy because of the deformities associated with it. It develops slowly, and the reasons for its spread are largely unknown. Leprosy is considered the least infectious of the contagious diseases known to affect humans. Fortunately, most people are naturally resistant to the disease, but among susceptible individuals in leprosy-endemic areas, contagiousness or communicability may be significant.[51]

Worldwide, at least twelve to fifteen million people are believed to suffer from HD. Most of them live in Asia, Central Africa, and Central and South America, in that order, where only about one person in five receives treatment. In the United States, there are approximately four thousand known leprosy cases, mostly in California, Florida, Hawaii, Louisiana, and Texas, where the endemic focus has been the ethnic communities of European immigrants. In 1981, Texas ranked fourth highest among states, with thirty-three new cases of HD. More than four hundred residents remain under observation or are being treated; most of them reside in coastal and southern counties, where over the past fifty years the pattern of occurrence has shifted to Hispanic communities.[52]

Since the early 1940s, sulfone drugs have been used to arrest the progress of leprosy by preventing the multiplication of *M. leprae*. Sulfones are safe, inexpensive, very stable, and are considered the drug of choice in spite of an ever-increasing problem of sulfone-resistant *M. leprae*. The current World Health Organization (WHO) recommendation is to treat all newly diseased patients with sulfones and one of the more recently developed antileprosy drugs to prevent the emergence of drug-resistant *M. leprae*. However, ultimately the best approach is prevention of the disease, and for this reason the development of a vaccine against leprosy is a high priority among leprologists throughout the world. To prepare a vaccine, however, a source of leprosy organisms is essential, and the discovery of the susceptibility of the nine-banded armadillo to leprosy provided that source.[53]

Over the past fifteen years North American armadillos have figured prominently because they assure an ample supply of bacilli from the most severe form, disseminated or lepromatous leprosy. Induced leprosy in armadillos has proved important for bacteriological, immunological, and epidemiological research.

In 1971, researchers at the Gulf South Research Institute at New Iberia, Louisiana, in collaboration with investigators at the National Hansen's Disease Center at Carville, Louisiana, reported successful transmission of leprosy to the armadillo. This animal has a normal body temperature of about 93°F, making it a suitable host for the microorganisms that can become established in the cooler parts of the human body, such as the ears and nose.

In addition to providing large numbers of leprosy bacilli, permitting the initiation of the WHO Immunology of Leprosy Program whose primary goal is the development of a vaccine to prevent leprosy, the armadillo could be used to prepare lepromin. Lepromin is a reagent that is used to assess the status of a patient already diagnosed with leprosy, allowing the clinician to project if a patient will develop the more benign form of leprosy (tuberculoid) or the more serious malignant lepromatous form. Lepromin is a suspension of heat-killed M. leprae that is injected into the skin of leprosy patients. Before the armadillo, the only source of bacilli was a patient with lepromatous leprosy, but the armadillo now provides the organism needed to prepare lepromin. In 1972, WHO designated the National Hansen's Disease Center at Carville as a reference center for the production of lepromin.[54]

Recent findings have demonstrated that North American armadillos are highly susceptible to M. leprae, certainly more so than humans. In tests, fully 80 percent of exposed animals contracted leprosy. Infected individuals usually carry higher loads of bacilli, are more likely to have diseased internal organs, and show shorter incubation periods (from six months to four years) than humans. The armadillo is the only established species that regularly develops disseminated or lepromatous leprosy and, therefore, is very suitable for evaluating new drugs for the treatment of this disease. The only other system for assaying the effect of new drugs is to use them on human patients, and an ethical question arises about whether a patient should be treated with an experimental drug that has not been first shown to be effective in an experimental model with the disease, such as the armadillo.[55]

In discussions about leprosy in armadillos, scientists have disagreed about two things: first, whether armadillos contract "real" leprosy, and whether they acquire this disease in the wild; second, if so, whether any of the more than two hundred people who contract leprosy annually in this country could have done so through handling armadillos.

In the first instance, some health officials have argued in the past that the armadillo's leprosy-like infection is not real leprosy. Most researchers, however, regard the experimental model of lepromatous leprosy in armadillos as *M. leprae*. Importantly, in 1974 investigators from the Gulf South Research Institute in New Iberia discovered a disease in a newly captured animal that was indistinguishable from that which results from inoculating armadillos with *M. leprae*. By 1981, 80 wild armadillos with indigenous leprosy had been identified. Seventy-nine came from about a dozen, mostly swampy, densely vegetated and insect-ridden locations in Louisiana, and a single infected animal was captured in northeastern Texas. Recent work in Texas involving 451 armadillos in fourteen coastal counties from East Texas to the Rio Grande Valley has shown a leprosy prevalence of 4.66 percent (similar to that in Louisiana), with variations from 2 to 15.4 percent. The Center for Disease Control in Atlanta, Georgia, also reported 1 diseased animal among 40 captured in southwest Mississippi.[56]

It is now agreed that the disease in wild-caught armadillos is indeed caused by *M. leprae*. And by all of the currently available criteria, the organism isolated from armadillos is identical to *M. leprae*. Recently the DNA from organisms isolated from naturally infected armadillos was compared to the DNA from human *M. leprae* and there was 100 percent homology, so there is no doubt that, according to the most advanced technology available, the organism is *M. leprae*.[57]

Experts believe that armadillos could have originally become infected by contact with contaminated bandages, clothing, etc., discarded by patients, who were carrying large numbers of very viable *M. leprae*, particularly before the use of sulfones. Authorities also know that *M. leprae* can survive in the environment for seven days or more, so immediate contact with the infected articles is not essential. Once the infection was introduced into the armadillo population, animal-to-animal transfer (mother to offspring, contaminated soil in burrows, insects, etc.) would have perpetuated the disease in this species.[58]

There is also ongoing debate about whether armadillos can infect humans with leprosy. A study by the Federal Center for Disease Control in Atlanta failed to show any association between leprosy patients in Louisiana and contact with nine-bandeds; but in 1979, the severe lepromatous form was diagnosed in an elderly Texan, a rancher and dairy farmer who had also hunted and trapped extensively, and included armadillo meat in his diet. Medical experts concluded that "one can be grateful that a taste for armadillo is not one of the most common food preferences." A very recent report implicates the handling of armadillos as the cause of leprosy in five patients in Texas. The men had had extensive contact with armadillos, and first lesions appeared on the hands and forearms where abrasions had occurred in the capture and handling of these sharp-clawed, sturdily built mammals.[59]

A number of interesting late-developing facts about armadillos and leprosy research include the successful human reaction to lepromins prepared from wild, diseased armadillos in Louisiana and used by leprosy research units and in places long distances from the infected armadillo sources. Furthermore, naturally acquired leprosy in a chimpanzee was reported in 1977 from an animal that had been purchased in Sierra Leone.[60] Another nonhuman primate, a mangabey monkey captured in Nigeria in about 1975, developed facial lesions in the United States in 1979. Suspensions of *M. leprae* from an armadillo with advanced lepromatous leprosy were injected into two healthy mangabey monkeys, and both animals showed lesions several months later. This fact "augments the evidence already provided by nine-banded armadillos and the chimpanzee that *M. leprae* can spontaneously cause lepromatous leprosy in non-human species." As monkeys are phylogenetically closely related to humans, studies of this mycobacterium in these species may provide the most relevant data to humans. For now, we can designate the nine-banded armadillo in the American South as "a reservoir for the disease" in the wild and as the model animal for the production of *M. leprae* and for other research immunology.[61]

While all health experts agree that more research is needed, more and more argue that it is "prudent to assume that there is some risk from handling or eating armadillos." In Texas, the Parks and Wildlife Code now officially restricts commerce in armadillos, supposedly to reduce the possibility of contracting diseases from them. But the law does not prohibit possessing armadillos for personal use or selling them to zoos or to scientific or medical institutions; as such, it is not likely to have much effect in reducing human contact with armadillos. In the international arena, projects sponsored by the World Health Organization in Geneva, Switzerland, that involve armadillos in leprosy research do not impose a heavy demand on animals nor are they likely to drain source regions in the American South.[62]

HUMANS AND ARMADILLO NUMBERS

Before World War II, armadillos were subjected to heavy hunting in order to satisfy the demand of curio dealers and people taking the animal for food. Armadillos were killed in such large numbers that biologist Vernon Bailey believed that they would be exterminated in Texas.[63]

Gentle outdoorsman Roy Bedichek noted how the "curious little beast was slaughtered mercilessly" as it scuttled northward. It was harassed not so much for its food value but, according to this naturalist, because of its reputation as destroying the nests of ground-dwelling birds. Sportsmen claimed that looting armadillos were killing off turkeys by feeding on their eggs, said Bedichek, who disliked hunters in general and scientists-turned-hunters especially. He scoffed at such claims, and charged that these men were concocting an "excuse for extending their killing range," to include harmless armadillos together with beneficial hawks and the "paisano" or roadrunner. This bird had also acquired the reputation of a nest destroyer.[64]

In recent decades, the armadillo has not been hunted so much. A few dozen shell baskets and mounted armadillos are made each year and sold from outlets in Central and Southeast Texas. In 1982, one dealer organized "the first major armadillo round-up since Texas turned chic," in order to procure twenty thousand dead animals. Advertisements in 120 Central Texas towns offered $2.50 for a frozen armadillo. The dealer obtained the quota after a month or two.[65]

Armadillo products figured in a recent sale of confiscated wildlife materials that had accumulated over a ten-year period. The sale, which was sponsored by the U.S. Fish and Wildlife Service, raised about $250,000 from across the nation, including $900 for nine handbags made of armadillo skins and $357.99 for "an armadillo guitar with broken strings."[66]

Automobiles and casual shooting compose the greatest threats to the armadillo. Some East Texas trappers may take a few animals during the fur-bearer season, but the number of armadillos they kill does not appear to be very large. Although there are no reliable estimates of the number of armadillos killed annually for food or supplied to research institutions, the number is not more than a few thousand per year. Research teams in the United States, Venezuela, Norway, and the United Kingdom, where about one hundred animals are delivered every two years for leprosy bacillus culture, do require a steady but small supply of animals. At present, armadillo populations can easily withstand these direct pressures from humans.

4. The Armadillo in Popular Culture

The rise of the armadillo to the status of "folk critter" began in the mid-1960s when Sam Lewis began to promote and popularize armadillo races at local carnivals and fundraising events in Texas towns. Ethnic foods, crafts, and sideshows, including cow chip tossing, hat stomping, and dunking booths, were spiced up when customers hired Lewis' armadillos for contests. Those visitors enjoyed themselves by yelling encouragement as they watched bemused animals scuttle along a short track.

In 1970, the entertainment value of armadillos received an extra boost with the opening of the Armadillo World Headquarters in Austin. Within two or three years this curious-looking mammal became special among musicians and enthusiasts of the concert hall's "Austin sound" that led progressive country music. By the close of the decade the armadillo had become very popular both as a harmless animal for people, especially youngsters, to have fun with, and as a symbol of a free and easy lifestyle for many urban teenagers and young adults. Entrepreneurs exploited this reflection of "laid-back," unconventional living by making armadillos an important element of what has been termed "Texas chic." So interested have Texans become in armadillos that in 1979 and again in 1981 resolutions were introduced into the Texas legislature to have the armadillo named the state mammal, placing it with other worthy mascots such as the mockingbird, the officially designated bird; the bluebonnet, the official flower; and the pecan, the state tree.[1]

ARMADILLO RACING

Sam Lewis is one of the most active promoters of armadillo races.[2] He has been involved in civic enterprises in San Angelo for many years, working hard to attract conventions and tourism to that West Texas town. In 1965, he thought up the idea of staging an armadillo race as a novelty that would attract public attention to San Angelo. The first few races were successful, and Lewis decided to expand his enterprise. With friends, he founded the World Armadillo Breeders and Racers Association (WABRA).

In the first few years, armadillo races were held in San Angelo in connection with a local festival, Concho Days. Racing soon became most popular in the event, and is now promoted as the World Armadillo Outdoor Racing Championship. This outdoor sprint has been associated with a similar gallop indoors through the lobby of the San Angelo Holiday Inn. In addition to work in San Angelo, Lewis transports armadillos throughout Texas and sends his charges to races out of state.

The objective of such races is to have the armadillos scuttle as fast as possible along a track just over 40 feet long and about 40 feet wide; an impressive 3.0-second dash in 1981 set the record. Some people regard armadillos as resembling speedy turtles in shell-to-shell contests, but enthusiasts in New Braunfels, 200 miles southeast of San Angelo, are not daunted by slow performances. In 1981, New Braunfels hosted the Armadillo Alympics, whose grand prize was a free trip to Hawaii for the winning trainer of the state champion.[3]

At armadillo races sponsored by WABRA, each entrant may either bring his or her own armadillo or rent one from the promoter's "racing stock." For contests in San Angelo, participants who intend to capture their own animals are given "armadillo hunting licenses" from the "Armadillo Control Commission." Most people, however, rent their armadillos, and Lewis attributes much of his success in promoting these races to a sizable stable of captive 'dillos just rarin' to be loosed down the chute. He frequently receives requests for advice from other race organizers and sponsors from across Texas who may be prepared to provide the facilities and trappings, but who expect contestants to provide their own armadillos. These races are usually not successful, according to Lewis, because few people are willing or able to enter their own fleet-footed armadillos.

One difficulty that Jaycees in Weslaco faced in their 1982 armadillo olympiad was a dearth of local animals. Rather than pay a hefty fee to the New Braunfels Racing Association, another group that supplies armadillos for olympics in various cities, and which had sent racers to Weslaco in 1981, the lower Valley residents planned to make a trip to the Hill Country in order to capture wild armadillos. Conditions for the race at Weslaco's Sugar Cane Festival had been so cold in February 1981 that the nine-bandeds were extremely reluctant to dash about. Moreover, catching wild armadillos in cold winter weather is a doubly daunting endeavor. The sugar festival's organizers had two problems: getting enough armadillos for their races, and satisfying animal lovers that such olympics are fun for armadillos.[4]

Sam Lewis and Associates offer to solve these kinds of logistical difficulties, and he makes plain his concern about treating armadillos humanely. Lewis transports his racing armadillos in plywood cages that fit into a van. The armadillos are given food and water for each trip—the standard diet that Lewis feeds to all of his captive animals—and prior to departure, a veterinarian examines them. For shipments into or through other states, health certificates are usually required. At WABRA races, the health and safety of every armadillo is of primary concern. For example, armadillos that are painted or covered with any foreign substance are not allowed to participate, and the owner of a disqualified animal is verbally chastised by both the "Chief Armadillo

Inspector" and the "Racing Commissioner." WABRA rules are strictly enforced and state that no drugs or other agents may be administered to the animals to make them run faster. Armadillo "trainers" may urge on their entrants by whistling, shouting, or beating the ground; but touching, pulling or pushing the animal, or using sticks as goads results in immediate disqualification. WABRA rules also insist that all animals entered in one of their events must be well cared for, so that the spirit of fun plus the threat of public and outspoken censure is sufficient in most cases to prevent mistreatment. Occasionally, some of Lewis' racing armadillos become "tired" and will neither race nor eat. These animals are reportedly returned and released in the wild where there are resident populations.

WABRA also promotes armadillo races across the nation. These events usually require permits in order to prevent the accidental introduction of armadillos into other parts of the country. Recently, for example, Lewis and his associates staged a race in southern California. He had to obtain entry permits for his stock from state wildlife officials, and a health certificate signed by a veterinarian was required for each animal. A state game warden inspected the armadillos on entry, noting the sex of each one; and at the end of the racing festivities, game authorities verified that the total number and the sex of the animals leaving the state tallied with those that had been checked earlier. Had one of the armadillos escaped, WABRA would have been responsible for its capture and would have been held liable for any expenses incurred in securing or killing the escapee. According to Lewis, there are similar requirements in other states, but not in those where the armadillo is a permanent resident.

GOING HOME WITH THE ARMADILLO

Since 1970, San Angelo has been promoted as the armadillo racing capital for Texas and the world. That same year also marked the beginning of Austin's rise to prominence as a national center for country music. The birthplace of what came to be known as the "Austin sound" was an old National Guard armory, a quonset hut converted to a concert hall and dubbed with the improbable name of Armadillo World Headquarters (AWHQ). Between its opening in August 1970 and its closing in December 1980, the Armadillo, or 'Dillo as it was affectionately called, gained an international reputation similar in some eyes to that of the Grand Ole Opry in Nashville or the Fillmore West in San Francisco. It attracted nationally recognized singers and musicians in rock and country music and launched new talent.[5]

Details about the colorful history of the Armadillo World Headquarters must be left to the chroniclers of contemporary rock and country music. Its relevance to this study lies in its role in popularizing the animal as a symbol of Texas, and in making people interested in and appreciative of real armadillos.

Credit for naming the cavernous hall that sat on just over half an acre of land goes to Eddie Wilson, one of the cofounders and first manager of the Armadillo World Headquarters. Wilson, who managed a local rock group, Shiva's Headband, joined with an attorney familiar with the San Francisco counterculture and two or three other local residents to rent for a modest fee this "shrine to the hippie entrepreneur." The Armadillo was an undistinguished brick building whose steel beams held up a corrugated tin roof over a concrete slab floor. Shiva's Headband, Ramon and the Four Daddy-Os, and the Hub City Movers performed when it opened its doors on August 7, 1970, and four years later in its heyday two hundred local musicians (mostly country-western) were involved with the institution.[6] Wilson later stated that the name "Armadillo" had no special meaning or significance, it just popped into his mind one day as he walked in downtown Austin. The choice was between that and "Uncle Zeke's Rock Emporium." But this explanation is not the stuff from which legends and folklore are made. Armed with a few facts about the armadillo's behavior and habits, local patrons and management, who displayed great enthusiasm rather than business acumen in the early years, developed an explanation for the name of the Armadillo which became the basis for the unwritten code of behavior for concert-goers.[7]

'Dillo regulars perceived the armadillo as an innocuous, unassuming little critter—independent, pleasant, and "laidback." In nature, the armadillo sometimes has the unusual habit of sharing its den with skunks, rabbits, and even rattlesnakes, and it is believed to tolerate these uninvited guests with little evidence of aggression or competition. It followed, then, that the Armadillo World Headquarters in the spirit of its animal namesake should accommodate, at least on a temporary basis, patrons of seemingly incompatible appearances, political persuasions, and lifestyles in the concert hall "den." On the occasion of the Armadillo's final performance on New Year's Eve 1980, long-time staffer and artist Micael Priest reflected upon the tolerant spirit of this Austin institution: "This was the headquarters," he said, "but y'all were the armadillos. I want you to continue to carry this throughout the country, to teach people how to have fun."[8]

ARMADILLO ART AND ARTIFACTS

The armadillo's odd appearance makes it a perfect subject for caricatures, and the concert hall's huge, sterile cinder block walls made the perfect tableau for creative expression. Jim Franklin, who has been called the "Michelangelo of armadillo art," is the person most responsible for making the armadillo "the totem animal of Austin." He was associated with the Armadillo World Headquarters from its opening, and when improvements were made to the old armory to include a second floor, he set up a studio there replete with mannequins, motorcyle parts, albums, flags, and wallhangings. This native son of La Marque, Texas, considered Austin a "magic city" because of the special kind of energy given off by the local Balcones Fault; armadillo decor doubt-less reflected that very special ambiance.⁹

Franklin claimed to have turned the armadillo from "a joke animal" to a symbol for the local underground through his drawings dating back to about 1968. His first rendition of the animal was for a handbill showing a "funky ol' arma-dillo smoking a joint." It was quickly followed by a map of Austin's interesting spots for *The Rag*, a local counter-culture paper, depicting nearsighted armadillos wandering along the streets seemingly oblivious of landmarks. Those first cartoons caught on and paved the way for the fad of armadilliana.¹⁰

Familiarity with the animal as offbeat had surfaced in the mid-1960s in the *Texas Ranger*, a well-established Univer-sity of Texas student publication. Artist Glen Whitehead's cartoon of a steam typewriter with editor Byron Black at the controls showed a small armadillo tied to the contraption. The magazine's logo sported a three-banded variety which, as an insert, began to appear in peculiar guises between mis-cellaneous jokes.

The University of Texas community in Austin was further introduced to the oddball armadillo through Franklin's work in the late sixties when local street vendors peddled a 36-page collection of his armadillo cartoons. Pictures squeezed animals from tubes of paint, turned them into po-lice helmets and other items. When the state legislature con-vened in 1969, Franklin produced what is probably his best-known illustration—an armadillo attempting to copulate with the dome of the state capitol. For several years Franklin had imagined that the capitol in Austin resembled the shell of a huge armadillo. Visitors could enter into the beast's body by walking along its tongue, through the mouth into the shell-like rotunda, and exit through the tapering tail. He imagined that this "superarmadillo" was a compelling siren for potential mates, hence the nine-banded's urge for inti-macy with the capitol.¹¹

With his reputation as the master of armadillo art already established, it was natural that Franklin should be selected to decorate the walls of the Armadillo World Headquarters. Decked out in his armadillo shell hat with antlers, Franklin turned the interior of the concert hall into what one local observer called the "Sistine Chapel of armadillo art."[12] Franklin also created the 'Dillo logo featuring a quartered globe of the earth encircled by four armadillos, and he worked as M.C. for early concerts. In the grande finale for the music hall on New Year's Eve 1980, Franklin made his final stage appearance in front of a painted panel of the Texas Hill Country and a Texas flag. He set up ten sections of tubing, and "with the audience counting from one to ten (one for each year of the hall's existence) he blew odd notes through the tube," and then he introduced Commander Cody, who welcomed in 1981.[13]

Two other artists, Micael Priest and Guy Juke, working for the Armadillo, displayed their talents in excellent posters promoting events in the music hall. Priest was art director for the Armadillo in 1975 and produced legible, comprehensive posters that could be hung "in a living-room situation." Juke may be best known for his illustration of Santa's sleigh pulled by eight large armadillos, used originally as an advertisement for the 1978 Annual Armadillo Christmas Vendor's Bazaar, when intensive efforts were well underway to keep the concert hall financially solvent.[14] In 1980, a larger-than-life model of the armadillo-drawn sleigh was constructed and suspended from the ceiling of the old armory building. When the Armadillo closed, the contents of the building, including furnishings and decoration, were sold by auction. Juke's sled with armadillos was snapped up by an adoring fan for $450.[15]

The 30,000-square-foot AWHQ was demolished in early 1981, and musicians and fans considered its passing the close of an era. The reason such performers as Waylon Jennings, Willie Nelson, Charlie Daniels, and scores of other country and rock music makers were regulars at the Armadillo lay in the audience response. Although it was never a financial success (being forced to file for Chapter 11 bankruptcy in federal court in 1977), the Armadillo received international acclaim because of the excellent rapport between artists and the public. Audience enthusiasm in such a funky den-like setting was highly contagious.[16]

More than 500 people registered to bid on the building's memorabilia in January 1981 and paid approximately $45,000 for an assortment of trophies, including a kitchen skillet "that had scraps of hamburger meat coagulated on it" and even a garbage can and its contents. Thousands stopped by to watch the men work on tearing down the empty building. Even in its death agony, the Armadillo den had surprises. "Pewee" Franks, owner of the demolition company, was reportedly astonished by the range of drug paraphernalia that his crew unearthed. Two final items, a small brass bell and a $20 gold certificate in the 1922 series, proved to be quite valuable.[17]

Today, the AWHQ site is part of a new "Texas Center," an all-too-common office, hotel, and parking lot cluster reaching across 7.5 acres. The Christmas bazaar, however, has continued to function for a couple of weeks every year under its old name in an old grocery store a few miles south of the hallowed space. In 1982 most of the old 'Dillo workers worked on the new premises, where customers could sip a beer as they checked out the eighty-three booths for gifts.[18]

Over the years, many local artists have produced all manner of illustrations, figurines, clothing, and stationery featuring the armadillo. Many of them hawk their wares from vendors' stalls located near the University of Texas campus in Austin. Others have outlets at local gift shops and department stores, or they have set up mail-order businesses—advertising armadillo art in periodicals such as *Texas Monthly* and *Southern Living*. Today, the list of armadillo-oriented arts and crafts is endless. Consumers have a wide range of stickers, decals, buttons, candles, trinkets, belt buckles, and T-shirts to choose from. Posters and drawings portraying the armadillo in lifelike reality as well as cartoonistic absurdity are in great demand and are among the more popular items of armadilliana.

"TEXAS CHIC"

The glorification of the armadillo has not been limited to artists and street people. In the late 1970s, stores specializing in merchandise with a "Texas flavor" discovered that "Texas sells." Their success in creating new markets has been attributed to the recent popularity of television programs, such as *Dallas*, movies like *The Best Little Whorehouse in Texas*, and novels and music about Texas and by Texans. Popular gifts in the 1980 Christmas season included fuzzy stuffed armadillos, taking the place of the traditional teddy bear, and a board game called "Armadillo Race."[19]

Even East Coast–based enterprises such as the prestigious magazine *Natural History* jumped on the armadillo bandwagon. Subscription reply cards in the January 1981 issue showed an armadillo standing on its hind legs with the caption "Here's an opportunity that won't cost you an armadillo and a leg."

But these gimmicks and advertising campaigns featuring armadillos pale in comparison to the media blitz put on by the Lone Star Brewing Company of San Antonio. Lone Star, which calls itself "the national beer of Texas," has used the armadillo in its advertising for several years, but no one on the current advertising staff can recall exactly how it got started. It seems that folks at Lone Star wanted something new and different, so they came up with the "giant armadillo." According to Lone Star's director of advertising, the idea for the "giant armadillo" came about because the company wanted a symbol that was "very Texan." Now, the Lone Star giant armadillo should not be confused with the *Priodontes giganteus* of South America. Rather, Lone Star's

"Ol' Blue" is, or rather was, an overgrown version of our old friend *Dasypus novemcinctus*. To satisfy his craving for "the national beer of Texas," "Blue" ambushed Lone Star beer trucks or broke into grocery stores and sucked up the supply of his favorite suds. The adventures of this marauding critter became so popular that even people who had never seen a real armadillo announced "I know about the armadillo," a line from one of Lone Star's TV commercials. In an effort to have more people know about the armadillo (and its product), Lone Star sponsored races throughout Texas, and also in Los Angeles, Phoenix, and St. Louis, and provided backing for the Armadillo World Headquarters, where the consumption of its beer reportedly gave the brewery its second largest account after Houston's Astrodome. In 1983 "Ol' Blue" was dropped after the purchase of Lone Star by Heileman of Wisconsin. Another brewery, however, has since included armadillos in TV advertising.[20]

By way of such events, the armadillo's popularity and notoriety as a symbol of Texas has spread far beyond the animal's current range and involves more than art. In 1981, Continental Airlines offered a cheap "armadillo fare" of $19.99 from Austin to El Paso, Houston, Midland-Odessa, and Lubbock. Sears stores offer armadillo chain link fencing and wooden Armadillo Matches made in Wadsworth, Ohio. As craftsman James Avery's brochure puts it, "The armadillo says Texas all the way."[21]

The phenomenal success of the "Capitol 10,000" long-distance race held annually in or near downtown Austin is due to the interest in health and fitness, and the armadillo has certainly assisted in this worthy cause sponsored by the *Austin American-Statesman* in cooperation with the city Parks and Recreation Department. The logo of an upstanding armadillo in jogging shoes and sunglasses has appeared regularly in promotional literature and on T-shirts. From its inception in 1978, this 10,000-meter race, called the "largest footrace in Texas," has always attracted curiously dressed teams and individuals, including coneheads and armadillos. The 1981 race drew a record 11,800 runners who started near the Capitol as a crowd six lanes across and three blocks deep. Finishers included children, an 81-year-old woman, and "a man disguised as an armadillo," and the race drew nationally recognized athletes and contestants from as far away as Chicago and Canada. First runners finished the 6.2-mile course in under thirty minutes while others came in more than two hours later. A record 14,248 entrants ran along hilly streets in 1982 to finish on the scenic shores of Town Lake. Again, armadillos were a keynote to this athletic happening, as they were in 1983, when more than 20,000 people ran and jogged along the course. Two large, two-man armadillos made the run and attracted attention from the media. In 1984 there were again over 20,000 entrants, including two "armadillos." One of these, made of cardboard and styrofoam and carried on the shoulders of two pilots from Dallas, finished in the first hour of the race, claiming "a world record for an armadillo."[22]

To help relieve traffic congestion and headaches from parking, a recent fleet of five Armadillo Express buses, resembling old trolley cars, have entered downtown thoroughfares in Austin. For 25 cents one can ride the "Dillo" from a free parking lot at the City Coliseum and meander northward into the central business district. Five hundred people used Austin's answer to San Francisco's cable cars on the first day in March 1984. City officials hope numbers will pick up so that this subsidized but convenient mode of travel will ease parking snafus while perking up riders. "We've got speakers in the cars and it's just a matter of time before we'll have that armadillo song that Willie Nelson sings playing in them," laughed Austin's public information director.[23]

THE STATE MAMMAL

In 1978, a group of students from Houston's Oak Creek Elementary School learned that Texas has an official state bird, flower, and tree, but no state mammal. Determined to alter this situation, the children drew up a list of potential candidates for the mammal that included the horned frog, the longhorn steer, the pronghorn antelope, and the nine-banded armadillo. After much debate, the armadillo was selected as the animal which best fit the image of Texas's official mammal. The Houston students convinced their state representative, Don Henderson, to sponsor a resolution to name the armadillo as the state mammal during the 1979 session of the state legislature. The resolution passed the House, but died in the Senate.[24]

Undaunted, the youngsters redoubled their efforts to have the resolution introduced during the 1981 session. First, they formed a loose-knit organization called "Armadillo in '81" made up chiefly of students, parents, teachers, and other armadillo supporters from the Houston area. This group organized support from other public schools, universities, and individuals across the state. Interestingly, sympathy for the animal also came from areas where the armadillo is not a resident, El Paso and Amarillo, for example, and from areas where the armadillo is uncommon. Representative Henderson was again recruited to sponsor the 1981 resolution (see Appendix).[25]

The resolution easily passed committee hearings. Pro-armadillo forces from Houston, Round Rock, and Austin prevailed, and the measure appeared to be on the way to easy passage before the full House. House debate, however, revealed some odd notions about the armadillo's ancestry. Representative David London of Bonham, who is not overly fond of the animal, asked, "Are you sure the armadillo is a mammal and not a cross between a mammal and a reptile?" Assured that armadillos are indeed mammals, London grumbled, "I still don't like armadillos." Representative Bennie Bock then voiced his opposition to the armadillo. Bock hails from New Braunfels, where, according to public sentiment, at times, it appears that armadillos have taken up

STATE TREE

STATE BIRD

STATE FLOWER

STATE MAMMAL

residence on every lawn and garden in town. "Why are you making that ugly pea-brained little creature or whatever it is the state mammal?" asked Bock, "I think we ought to just kill 'em all, we've got a lot of famous animals other than a little bitty thing that just doesn't count for nothing." But resolution opponents, while vocal, were neither especially articulate nor well organized; HCR 53 passed the House by voice vote and was sent to the Senate.[26]

At first, it looked as if the resolution would not even be considered in the Senate. The session was nearing the end of its constitutionally mandated time, and opposition to the resolution developed as in 1979. Jack Ogg, the Senate sponsor, also from Houston, sought a compromise by offering a substitute resolution which would have given the armadillo status as the "recognized mascot of Texas." Ogg's resolution was placed on the Senate's "local" calendar, where it was expected to pass along with a number of other uncontested resolutions. The opposition recognized Ogg's maneuver, however, and Senator Bob Vale of San Antonio, who was quoted as saying, "I'm against the armadillo being named the official anything," succeeded in pulling the resolution from the calendar.[27] Later, pro-armadillo forces in the Senate began behind-the-scenes wrangling so that the Ogg compromise resolution was again placed on the calendar two days before adjournment. However, opposition in the Senate was too well organized and the resolution was defeated.

There appears to be no single point of opposition among anti-armadillo advocates. The animal has received bad press over the years, and some opponents have continued to argue that it feasts on the eggs of quail and other ground-nesting birds. In some parts, the armadillo is considered a pest because it roots and digs into lawns and gardens; this would explain the lack of support from Bock, London, Vale, and others from armadillo-"infested" districts.

Curiously, had HCR 53 passed, the armadillo would not have been afforded any measure of protection. The resolution included no prohibitions against hunting or racing armadillos, using their meat, or manufacturing curios from their shells. In short, Texans could have continued to persecute the animal. In this way, the proponents of HCR 53 cleverly avoided the issue of government interference with the rights of citizens so far as armadillos are concerned. It appears, then, that the general political climate in Austin was responsible for the defeat of the resolution more than any other factor. The state legislature has been often criticized for devoting too much time to frivolous and unnecessary issues while neglecting more important business, and the armadillo resolution was the so-called "biennial legislative joke" in the state capitol (one aide described it as giving "us more grief than redistricting").[28] The resolution twice passed the House, where some anonymity is afforded supporters in a voice vote, but failed in the smaller Senate, whose members appear to be more sensitive to charges of taking up non-essential matters.

The pro-armadillo faction gained some measure of success again in October 1981, when Senator Ogg, serving as president pro tempore of the Senate, was sworn in as "Governor for a day." Ogg used his status to declare the armadillo the "official state mascot" by executive decree. This designation affords no special status or protection to the animal. Indeed, some people think that this compromise action may have effectively diluted the efforts for the state mammal designation. Senator Ogg's action, however, lent some official recognition to the mammal and has elevated the armadillo to a position symbolizing "the attributes that distinguish a true Texan" (HCR 53).[29]

An institutional fillip for the armadillo came on December 5, 1982, which Governor Bill Clements declared as "Armadillo Safety Day." This proclamation coincided with the First Ever Great Armadillo Birthday Party (some said it was the 300 millionth) held in Fredericksburg. Despite scouring the hills, sponsors turned up only a few real armadillos, so they made do with broomsticks with wooden armadillo heads tacked on. Nevertheless, author James Michener, who includes armadillos in his book about Texas, sent his regards, and the sundry toys, belt buckles, and miniature six-packs of Lone Star beer labeled as "bait," plus live music, helped keep up interest and added to the conviviality.[30]

ECOLOGICAL CONSIDERATIONS

To date, recent cultural events involving the armadillo have not exerted any limiting effect on local populations. The relocation of some animals and the introduction of others into new territories as a result of these activities appears likely. Full-time racing promoters such as Sam Lewis report that they take only a few armadillos at a time from specific areas where animals appear to be common. And at the end of their racing careers, or if they refuse to run, the animals are usually released, although there are exceptions. For example, the Weslaco Sugarfest that planned an armadillo round-up in the Hill Country 300 miles away expected to release armadillos in the local area. Other animals are kept as "pets," but they may escape or be released when the novelty of owning one of these unusual mammals wears off. Thus, it is not uncommon for armadillos to be moved from one part of Texas to another.

It seems certain that with the current infatuation with the armadillo, some animals will be carried into new areas where they are not yet established. In the past few years, many people moving to Texas from other states have been caught up in the armadillo craze. One person with whom we are acquainted is determined to spread the armadillo in his home state of South Carolina. Armadillo-related events are very popular at college campuses in Texas, and as the state has a sizable out-of-state student population, the probability of introductions and possible range extension seems high.

5. Armadillos Forever

The first armadillos that entered the lower Rio Grande Valley of Texas in the 1840s and 1850s were early pioneers in the invasion from a well-established range in Mexico and Central America. The possibility exists that some individuals were carried across the Rio Grande into Texas as pets or to be used as food by settlers. Several early reports indicate that people kept armadillos captive and ate their meat.[1]

Once established, the nine-banded armadillo expanded its range in South Texas, so that by 1905 it occupied most of that brush country and had moved into the Edwards Plateau. At least four isolated populations existed well beyond the main area of distribution, lending indirect support to the argument that range extension was possibly assisted by humans. By the 1920s, the armadillo had moved into East Texas, had crossed the Sabine River into Louisiana, and, farther north, had found its way into southern Arkansas. During the 1930s, moving along the valleys of the Red and Arkansas rivers, a few animals were reported in Oklahoma.

The armadillo's pattern of distribution in its home base of Texas has remained fairly stable over the past thirty years. It is found in all parts except in the Trans-Pecos and High Plains, where normally arid conditions preclude its establishment as a permanent resident. In Louisiana, armadillos do not occur in the wet bayou and delta country bordering the Gulf Coast, but have colonized the remainder of the state. Recent reports suggest that nine-bandeds continue to move northward in Oklahoma and in Arkansas, and they have been seen in additional counties in both states within the past fifteen years. Population densities are low in northern parts of Oklahoma and Arkansas, but animals are breeding and numbers are reportedly increasing or at least holding their own. Notice of armadillos has come from additional states, such as Colorado, Kansas, and Missouri; however, by 1978, breeding was reported only in Kansas.

East of the Mississippi River, armadillos have become established in at least three states—Mississippi, Alabama, and Florida—from having been released or by escaping from captivity. In the first two states this happened fifty or more years ago, and in both cases movement northward is continuing. Range extension, however, has not been as rapid as one would have expected from comparisons with states to the west.

In Florida, two pairs of captive armadillos escaped in the 1920s and began to reproduce, spreading from the Cocoa Beach locality on the East Coast. After about twenty years, animals had spread throughout the Florida peninsula except the Everglades. They continued to press northward into Georgia and westward into the Florida Panhandle. Individuals from Alabama have spread into the western Panhandle of Florida, although as recently as the early 1970s, the eastern "Florida" group remained cut off from the western or "Texas"-based group. By 1978, however, the unoccupied gap in the central Florida Panhandle had narrowed considerably, and the discontinuity is now closed. Another "bridge" between the eastern and western groups has been fashioned in southwestern Georgia.

One report has noted a large number of "pioneers" on the coastal plain in Georgia, and our 1978 survey confirmed that these animals are becoming established. A single individual in Troup County suggests that range extension in the Georgia piedmont is continuing.[2]

Armadillos have also been reported from Tennessee and South Carolina during the past decade. However, no resident animals turned up in the 1978 survey. Still, it appears to be only a matter of time until both states are included in this mammal's range, either by way of natural pioneering or through human introductions.[3]

In the west, the armadillo's movements are blocked by aridity. Its western limit in Texas is a zone of marginal habitat, dry lands where population densities are low and distribution is discontinuous. Isolated numbers occur where there is available food and water; and in years of above average rainfall, these animal pioneers are seen in the Trans-Pecos and Panhandle regions of Texas, and move along the Pecos River Valley into New Mexico; but breeding in these areas is not favored on a permanent basis.

Our recent surveys confirm that armadillo numbers in West Texas fluctuate and those in northern areas seem to be stable, even after the severe winters of 1976–1977 and 1977–1978. However, record cold waves in January 1982 and December 1983 may have adversely affected numbers in northern Oklahoma and in Arkansas. Animals can live out cold weather in dens well insulated with leaf and grass litter, several feet underground. But the problem of searching for food remains. Insects and other edible organisms have been discovered in sizable numbers in Texas dens, so that it is possible that armadillos can subsist on such adventitious food sources, but for how long is uncertain.[4]

How far north can we expect America's nine-banded armadillo to spread eventually? In the past, opinions have positioned a "cold threshold," across which animals will not normally survive, too far to the south. Forty or fifty years ago this imaginary east-west line just about followed the 34th parallel. Currently, west of the Mississippi River, armadillos reproduce regularly beyond 36°N latitude and are reportedly forging toward the 37th parallel.

But if one looks for clues in the animal's corresponding range in the southern hemisphere, one thing is clear—the armadillo is not specialized for cold western living. At least five other armadillos, of which at least one has been found to hibernate, occur south of Buenos Aires in Argentina, or about 35°S, which approximates the limit for *D. novemcinctus* in South America. The nine-banded armadillo has adapted to winter cold in North America better than early experts predicted, but in South America it has colonized neither the Pampas south of about Buenos Aires nor the cold altiplano upland in the Andean Cordillera, where another armadillo resides.[5]

Therefore, the march northward in North America will become more like a crawl, into those special localities where ameliorating factors such as aspect, vegetation cover, and food supplies make winters tolerable. In the near future, the spread northward through variegated habitats east of the Mississippi River all the way to the Atlantic Coast piedmont in the Carolinas can be expected to "catch up" with earlier colonization in Arkansas, Missouri, and Kansas.

On the other hand, the armadillo copes well with hot, moist, broad-leaved, evergreen-forest localities, in the Amazon Basin, for example. It also breeds in thorn brushlands and in mesic woodlands, preferring riparian areas, in northern parts of its range. This "generalist" characteristic of the nine-banded armadillo is confirmed by one author who also calls it "arid-adapted"; that is, it can survive where water is scarce, but is not a true desert mammal. If it were, Californians rather than Texans might perhaps have developed a fondness for the scuttling creatures. If it had managed to penetrate the Sonoran Desert into southern California from a foothold in Sinaloa, perhaps residents would have placed it and not their extinct grizzly bear on state insignia. Armadillos have not scurried through the dryland belt of northern Mexico, at least not on a permanent basis. Texans have discovered that nine-bandeds don't thrive or even survive for very long in regions of high moisture deficits, such as the Trans-Pecos and High Plains.[6]

In sum, the nine-banded armadillo is a very adaptable

mammal. It has colonized a variety of habitats, including ones heavily modified by human activities. But it does not have the qualities of a specialist that lives by hibernation in very cold regions, nor the water-retaining efficiencies needed for the very dry ones. Other armadillo species possess these special characteristics much better than the nine-banded, but that is why they remain on the southern margins of the nine-banded's enormous range.

Humans have hunted armadillos from the beginning in the United States. Texans slaughtered them by the thousands, especially between 1900 and 1940, in order to clear pastures of such burrowing "varmints," to free ground-nesting birds from predatory activities, and to supply the demand for curios made from the animals' shells. These pressures brought about significant declines in local populations and led Vernon Bailey to speculate in 1930 that the armadillo was being hunted to extinction in Texas. Fortunately for the armadillo, the interest in shell baskets and other knickknacks made from the skins declined after World War II. A few animals continue to be killed and mounted or made up into baskets. Sam Lewis, for example, sells a dozen or two from his shop in San Angelo every year. In the past few years, state wildlife biologists have noticed that some trappers in East Texas are offering armadillo shells for sale. As yet, the number taken for such purposes is not large.[7]

Pest control operations involving the extermination of armadillos are not widespread, nor are they sustained, but some people in both the 1978 and 1981 surveys suggested that the armadillo can be a local menace to crops and gardens. Control measures are not always effective because the animal is neither trapped easily nor attracted to poisoned baits; shooting with a small caliber rifle is the convenient way of killing such crop- or lawn-damaging individuals.

The armadillo has been and continues to be a source of food in several southern states. The custom of eating its flesh is not always considered acceptable, however. Some residents continue to hold to an old folk belief that armadillos burrow into human graves and therefore are not fit for human consumption.[8] What is more likely to be true is that people are discouraged by the animal's odd appearance and its objectionable musky odor. There have also been some expressions of concern about the possibility of contracting leprosy from infected armadillos. Nevertheless, barbecued armadillo and armadillo chili remain popular at festivals and cook-off contests in Texas.

The armadillo has figured prominently in medical and scientific research for decades. Research institutions have been unable to breed the animal in captivity on a sustained basis, thereby necessitating the purchase of stock from suppliers. The number of animals needed for medical research is not great, but the practice of shipping armadillos from one part of the country to another increases the likelihood of accidental introductions. The discovery that the diagnostic reagent lepromin can be derived from armadillos infected with the leprosy bacillus should not result in a greatly increased demand for the animals, since a single armadillo provides enough material for more than 1,000 units of lepromin.

Before the mid-1960s, most people had ambivalent feelings about the armadillo. Farmers and ranchers ignored it or considered it an agricultural pest; hunters blamed armadillos for predation and often shot them on sight. Curio dealers thought of the armadillo only as material for baskets and other items made from its shell. But after about 1965, armadillo racing started to become popular in fairs and festivals throughout Texas. Interest in this offbeat form of entertainment has spread to other states, thereby increasing the possibility of armadillos being released into new areas notwithstanding the precautions taken by state officials.

In the past decade or so, the armadillo has come to represent the relaxed lifestyle of artists, musicians, and fans of the "Austin sound." Efforts to promote Texas and the Sun

Belt have propelled the armadillo to "folk critter" status—it symbolizes Texas and Texans. Big budget advertising combined with an array of gifts, games, trinkets, T-shirts, and art work featuring the armadillo has stirred up popular interest in the animal in many parts of the country. In 1979 and again in 1981, unsuccessful efforts were launched to name the armadillo the "state mammal of Texas."

Promotional knickknacks reflect more than merely cashing in on a fad for armadillos. Conservation of non-game animals, of which the armadillo is an example, is receiving more support from the public than ever before. It is inconceivable that such a popular interest would have been expressed about an animal lacking obvious material values fifty or even twenty years ago. Today, however, there is a lively debate about observing animals rather than consuming them by hunting. More people argue that animals have an intrinsic right to exist and should be respected beyond the economic benefits they supply. Questions about animal rights and the treatment of organisms are being discussed in the media as never before.

The plight of the California condor and that of the whooping crane are well-recognized conservation issues; the status and spread of the nine-banded armadillo is an element in the interest about the ecology and life histories of the plant and animal kingdoms. In rejecting the "meat and trophy" concept as too limiting, care must be expressed to keep from cosseting these animals and bringing them to a state of tameness or so-called domestication. People are committed to the survival of rare species and of non-game animals and birds because they perceive them as interesting, colorful, and different in their own right—sources of genetic diversity that have more appeal to the mind than to the stomach. This attitude may indeed reflect the bias of urban rather than rural residents.

The same urban people may regard armadillos as Texans par excellence and demand the trinkets that surround such an animal with the qualities of an "anti-hero." But there is something more under that entrepreneurial glint, and that is the satisfaction the public enjoys in observing animals. This may be exemplified in a safari park or a wilderness area, and it is what Roy Bedichek wrote about in his books celebrating the humble plants and animals in Texas. There exists a unity and bondedness among living things, and by being quiet and watchful each one of us can sense that belonging. The armadillo, like the state-recognized mockingbird and bluebonnet, strikes a responsive chord. It contributes to what geographers call the "personality" of a region. Its presence adds to the sense of place, and as such it becomes a vital link in the chain that binds life and land—our common heritage.

Appendix
House Concurrent Resolution
No. 53

Whereas, The great State of Texas has previously adopted an official bird, tree, flower, and food; it is now appropriate that we join other states in choosing a state mammal; and,

Whereas, This resolution has been prepared by the students of Oak Creek Elementary School in Harris County representing the students and children of Texas who all agree that the nine-banded armadillo, whose skin is as tough as a cowboy's boot, should be the official mammal of Texas; and,

Whereas, The armadillo is a hardy, pioneering creature that chose to begin migrating here about the time Texas became a state; and,

Whereas, The armadillo possesses many remarkable and unique traits, some of which parallel the attributes that distinguish a true Texan, such as a deep respect and need for the land, the ability to change and adapt, and a fierce, undying love for freedom; and,

Whereas, The students of Oak Creek Elementary School found a fact of interest representing each band of the armadillo as follows:

1. Like many residents of the great State of Texas, the armadillo prefers the days of sunshine and warmth to those of freezing temperatures;

2. The armadillo's sense of smell can warn him of danger or lead him to lunch as quickly as a Texan can sniff out a barbeque or a chili cook-off;

3. The hide and armor of the armadillo make him tough and unafraid of brambles, thorns, and rough terrain;

4. When startled, the armadillo can move as fast as a running back from the Oilers or the Cowboys (his fine reputation as a racer is well known);

5. The armadillo is an excellent burrow builder, and just as Texans provide homes for refugees from northern states, the armadillo generously vacates his burrow so that other creatures may have shelter;

6. Unperturbed by water, the armadillo can walk on a creek bed under the water or float across the creek, whichever he chooses to be appropriate;

7. Proving his usefulness to man, the armadillo, as a research animal, holds the key to the cure of leprosy, and he also labors to rescue Texas from the fire ant by eating every one he finds;

8. Carrying on the fine tradition of Texans as goodwill ambassadors around the world, four West Texas armadillos have recently set up housekeeping in the Peking, China, zoo;

9. And, finally, the armadillo reflects the good humor of the residents of Texas who proudly display his likeness on T-shirts, belt buckles, and pickup truck windows; now, therefore, be it

Resolved by the House of Representatives of the State of Texas, the Senate concurring, That the 67th Legislature hereby proclaim the Nine-Banded Armadillo, Dasypus novemcinctus mexicanus, as the official mammal of the State of Texas.

Notes

INTRODUCTION

1. Gilbert T. Crosby, "Spread of the Cattle Egret in the Western Hemisphere," *Bird Banding* 43 (July 1972): 205–212; John L. Long, *Introduced Birds of the World*, pp. 217–218.

1. THE NATURAL HISTORY OF ARMADILLOS

1. Wilma George, *Animal Geography*, pp. 74–78; Terry A. Vaughan, *Mammalogy*, p. 131.
2. Ernest P. Walker, *Mammals of the World*, 3d ed., 1: 492, 496.
3. Karen McBee and Robert J. Baker, "Dasypus novemcinctus," *Mammalian Species* no. 162 (1982): 6.
4. Walker, *Mammals* 1: 498; Walburga Moeller, "Edentates," in *Grzimek's Animal Life Encyclopedia* 11: 161.
5. David H. Greegor, "Renal Capabilities of an Argentine Desert Armadillo," *Journal of Mammalogy* 56 (1975): 626.
6. Walker, *Mammals* 1: 493.
7. Ibid., p. 494.
8. Ibid., p. 495.
9. Ibid., pp. 501, 502.
10. Ibid., p. 496; Charles Palmer, personal communication, December 12, 1982.
11. Moeller, "Edentates," p. 157; Ralph M. Wetzel and Edgardo Mondolfi, "The Subgenera and Species of Long-Nosed Armadillos, Genus *Dasypus* L.," in *Vertebrate Ecology in the Northern Neotropics*, ed. John F. Eisenberg, pp. 45, 46.
12. Vaughan, *Mammalogy*, p. 138; Walker, *Mammals* 1: 500.
13. Campbell and Lynn Loughmiller, eds., *Big Thicket Legacy*, pp. 138–139; J. Frank Dobie, "Hoover Hogs," *Frontier Times* 36 (1961): 32; Coleman C. Newman and Rollin H. Baker, "Armadillo Eats Young Rabbits," *Journal of Mammalogy* 23 (1942): 450; J. Frank Dobie, "The Armadillo Gets the Milk," *Austin American-Statesman*, November 16, 1958.

14. Edward R. Kalmbach, *The Armadillo: Its Relation to Agriculture and Game*, pp. 56–58.

15. William K. Clark, "Ecological Life History of the Armadillo in the Eastern Edwards Plateau Region" (M.A. thesis, University of Texas, 1949), p. 64.

16. Ibid., p. 33.

17. John F. Eisenberg, "Observation on the Nest Building Behavior of Armadillos," *Proceedings of the Zoological Society of London* 137 (1961): 323; Clark, "Ecological Life History," p. 42.

18. Clark, "Ecological Life History," p. 39.

19. James N. Layne and Debbie Glover, "Home Range of the Armadillo in Florida," *Journal of Mammalogy* 58 (1977): 411–413.

20. J. D. Mitchell to Vernon Bailey, March 25, 1915, Record Unit 7176, U.S. Fish and Wildlife Service, Field Reports, Box 95, Folder 7, Smithsonian Institution Archives.

21. William B. Davis, *The Mammals of Texas*, p. 270.

22. Ibid.; Eleanor E. Storrs, "The Astonishing Armadillo," *National Geographic* 161 (1982): 820.

23. Davis, *The Mammals of Texas*, p. 270.

24. Kathryn Apelt Jorns, interview, October 9, 1980.

25. F. Wallace Taber, "Extension of the Range of the Armadillo," *Journal of Mammalogy* 20 (1939): 489–490; Henry S. Fitch, Phil Goodrum, and Coleman Newman, "The Armadillo in the Southeastern United States," *Journal of Mammalogy* 33 (1952): 22.

26. G. D. Buchanan and Roy V. Talmage, "The Geographical Distribution of the Armadillo in the United States," *Texas Journal of Science* 6 (1954): 147–148.

27. Kalmbach, *The Armadillo*, p. 21; Troy L. Best, Barbara Hoditschek, and Howard H. Thomas, "Foods of Coyotes (*Canis latrans*) in Oklahoma," *Southwestern Naturalist* 26 (1981): 67–69.

28. Joel Asaph Allen, "On Mammals Collected in Bexar County and Vicinity, Texas," *Bulletin of the American Museum of Natural History* 8 (April 1896): 47–80.

29. Valgene Lehmann, *Forgotten Legions: Sheep in the Rio Grande Plain of Texas*, pp. 79–81, 97.

30. Danny Swepston, *The Status of the Armadillo in Texas*, p. 2; Stephen R. Humphrey, "Zoogeography of the Nine-Banded Armadillo (*Dasypus novemcinctus*) in the United States," *BioScience* 24 (1974): 458; Kalmbach, *The Armadillo*, pp. 21–22.

31. Valgene Lehmann, "Armadillo Investigations" (notes from a 1939 survey); Fitch, Goodrum, and Newman, "The Armadillo," p. 25.

32. Henry P. Attwater to Edward Preble, May 17, 1929, Record Unit 7252, Edward Alexander Preble Papers, Box 1, Folder 8, Smithsonian Institution Archives.

33. William Lloyd, "Mammals of the Lower Rio Grande," Special Reports, 1890, Record Unit 7176, U.S. Fish and Wildlife Service, Field Reports, pp. 2–3, Box 94, Folder 18, Smithsonian Institution Archives.

34. Clark, "Ecological Life History," p. 26; Fitch, Goodrum, and Newman, "The Armadillo," p. 28.

35. Layne and Glover, "Home Range," p. 413.

36. F. Wallace Taber, "Contribution on the Life History and Ecology of the Nine-Banded Armadillo," *Journal of Mammalogy* 26 (1945): 214–216.

37. Vernon Bailey, "Texas: Kerrville to Rock Springs, July 1–August 1, 1902," Record Unit 7176, U.S. Fish and Wildlife Service, Field Reports, Box 92, Folder 24, Smithsonian Institution Archives.

38. William K. Clark, "Ecological Life History of the Armadillo in the Eastern Edwards Plateau Region," *American Midland Naturalist* 46 (1951): 353.

39. Taber, "Contribution on Life History," p. 215.

40. Ibid., pp. 215–216; Swepston, *The Status of the Armadillo*, p. 1, and personal communication, March 23, 1981.

41. Taber, "Contribution on Life History," pp. 214–215.

42. Wilfred T. Neill, "The Spread of the Armadillo in Florida," *Ecology* 33 (1952): 284.

43. Miklos D. F. Udvardy, *Dynamic Zoogeography*, pp. 166–167.

44. Kjell Johansen, "Temperature Regulation in the Nine-Banded Armadillo," *Physiological Zoology* 34 (1961): 126–144.

45. Kalmbach, *The Armadillo*, p. 7; Fitch, Goodrum, and Newman, "The Armadillo," pp. 26–27.

46. Johansen, "Temperature Regulation," pp. 130–131.

47. Jorns, interview, October 9, 1980.

48. Frank Weaker, interview, March 12, 1981.

49. Buchanan and Talmage, "Geographical Distribution," p. 148.

50. Kalmbach, *The Armadillo*, p. 7.

51. Greegor, "Renal Capabilities," pp. 630–631.

52. Taber, "Contribution on Life History," pp. 215, 219; Clark, "Life History" (1951), pp. 343–345, 358.

53. Vernon Bailey, *Biological Survey of Texas*, p. 54; H. H. Newman, "The Natural History of the Nine-Banded Armadillo of Texas," *American Naturalist* 47 (1913): 518; Taber, "Contribution on Life History," p. 214.

54. Humphrey, "Zoogeography," pp. 458–459.

2. DISTRIBUTION AND DISPERSAL IN THE SOUTH

1. Henry S. Fitch, Phil Goodrum, and Coleman Newman, "The Armadillo in the Southeastern United States," *Journal of Mammalogy* 33 (1952): 21–37.
2. Vernon Bailey, *Biological Survey of Texas*, p. 53.
3. Benjamin F. Lundy, *The Life, Travels, and Opinions of Benjamin Lundy*, p. 152; Viktor Bracht, *Texas in 1848*, trans. C. F. Schmidt, p. 45.
4. John James Audubon and John Bachman, *Quadrupeds of North America* 3: 224–225.
5. Edward Drinker Cope, "On the Zoological Position of Texas," *Bulletin of the U.S. National Museum* 17 (1880): 10.
6. Donald E. Everett, *San Antonio: The Flavor of Its Past, 1845–1898*, p. 69.
7. Edwin T. Dumble, "The Armadillo (*Tatusia peba*) in Texas," *American Naturalist* 26 (1892): 72; Joel Asaph Allen, "On Mammals Collected in Bexar County and Vicinity, Texas," *Bulletin of the American Museum of Natural History* 8 (April 1896): 51.
8. Bailey, *Biological Survey of Texas*, p. 55.
9. Ibid., p. 53; Harry Oberholser, "Texas: Laredo Mammals," May 1901, Record Group 7176, U.S. Fish and Wildlife Service, Field Reports, Box 95, Folder 16, Smithsonian Institution Archives.
10. Bailey, *Biological Survey of Texas*, pp. 52, 53, 55.
11. Ibid., pp. 16, 23–26, 33.
12. Ibid., p. 54.
13. Ibid., pp. 53–54.
14. Campbell and Lynn Loughmiller, eds., *Big Thicket Legacy*, pp. 138–139.
15. John K. Strecker, "Notes on the Fauna of a Portion of the Canyon Region of Northwestern Texas," Baylor Bulletin 13 (1910): 21–22.
16. In November 1978, questionnaire surveys were mailed to 144 selected county agriculture agents in Texas, New Mexico, Oklahoma, Arkansas, Kansas, Missouri, Louisiana, Tennessee, Mississippi, Alabama, Georgia, Florida, and South Carolina. In March 1981, a similar follow-up survey was mailed to 87 wildlife biologists to update information collected in 1978. Some questionnaire respondents were contacted individually during 1982 and early 1983 to verify details about the status of armadillos in selected localities, particularly areas along the western and northern mar-

gins of the armadillo's range. Survey questions dealt with the appearance or disappearance of armadillos from an area during the preceding five years, habitat preferences, local population densities, agents of mortality, and human use of armadillos.

17. Ibid.
18. Danny Swepston, *The Status of the Armadillo in Texas*, p. 1, and personal communication, March 23, 1981.
19. Fitch, Goodrum, and Newman, "The Armadillo," pp. 23–24.
20. W. Frank Blair, "The Nine-Banded Armadillo in Northeastern Oklahoma," *Journal of Mammalogy* 17 (1936): 293–294; S. C. Dellinger and J. D. Black, "Notes on Arkansas Mammals," *Journal of Mammalogy* 21 (1940): 187–191; F. Wallace Taber, "Extension of the Range of the Armadillo," *Journal of Mammalogy* 20 (1939): 489–493.
21. G. D. Buchanan and Roy V. Talmage, "The Geographical Distribution of the Armadillo in the United States," *Texas Journal of Science* 6 (1954): 142–150.
22. A. G. Cleveland, "The Current Geographic Distribution of the Armadillo in the United States," *Texas Journal of Science* 22 (1970): 90–92.
23. Ibid.; C. R. Wenger, "The Amazing Armadillo," *Arkansas Game and Fish* 9 (Winter 1977): 8–10.
24. James H. Barnes, Washita County (Oklahoma) Extension Director, reply to our 1978 survey.
25. H. H. Bailey, "The Armadillo in Florida and How It Reached There," *Journal of Mammalogy* 5 (1924): 264–265; Wilfred T. Neill, "The Spread of the Armadillo in Florida," *Ecology* 33 (1952): 282–284.
26. Fitch, Goodrum, and Newman, "The Armadillo," p. 24; G. D. Buchanan, "The Current Range of the Armadillo *Dasypus novemcinctus mexicanus* in the United States," *Texas Journal of Science* 10 (1958): 349–351; Cleveland, "Current Geographic Distribution," pp. 91–92.
27. Stephen R. Humphrey, "Zoogeography of the Nine-Banded Armadillo (*Dasypus novemcinctus*) in the United States," *BioScience* 24 (1974): 457–460.
28. Fitch, Goodrum, and Newman, "The Armadillo," pp. 25–26.
29. Buchanan and Talmage, "Geographical Distribution," p. 146.
30. Cleveland, "Current Geographic Distribution," p. 91; our surveys, 1978 and 1983.
31. Fitch, Goodrum, and Newman, "The Armadillo," p. 26; Taber, "Extension of the Range," pp. 491–492.

32. Fitch, Goodrum, and Newman, "The Armadillo," p. 26; Cleveland, "Current Geographic Distribution," pp. 91–92.
33. Humphrey, "Zoogeography," p. 457.
34. Vernon Bailey, *Mammals of New Mexico*, p. 8.
35. L. Joseph Hendricks, "Observation of Armadillo in East-Central New Mexico," *Journal of Mammalogy* 44 (1963): 581; Jack W. Schaefer, *An American Bestiary*, p. 133.
36. Humphrey, "Zoogeography," p. 458.
37. Eleanor E. Storrs, "The Astonishing Armadillo," *National Geographic* 161 (1982): 827.
38. Albert E. Sanders, "Order Edentata," in *An Annotated Checklist of the Biota of the Coastal Zone of South Carolina*, ed. Richard G. Zingmark, p. 299.
39. V. Bailey, *Biological Survey of Texas*, p. 54; H. H. Newman, "The Natural History of the Nine-Banded Armadillo of Texas," *American Naturalist* 47 (1913): 518; Buchanan and Talmage, "Geographical Distribution," pp. 148–149.
40. Humphrey, "Zoogeography," pp. 458–459.
41. Buchanan and Talmage, "Geographical Distribution," pp. 143–146; Buchanan, "Current Range," pp. 349–350; Humphrey, "Zoogeography," p. 457–467; Cleveland, "Current Geographic Distribution," p. 91; our 1978 and 1981 surveys.
42. Humphrey, "Zoogeography," p. 459.

3. HUMAN USE OF THE ARMADILLO

1. Unless otherwise noted, details about operations at the Apelt Armadillo Company are from an interview with Kathryn Apelt Jorns in Austin, October 9, 1980.
2. H. H. Newman, "The Natural History of the Nine-Banded Armadillo of Texas," *American Naturalist* 47 (1913): 513–539.
3. Charles Apelt is first listed on Kerr County Tax Rolls in 1888; in 1891 he is recorded as owning property worth $1,830, including three horses, two cattle, and two hogs; see Kerr County Tax Assessor, "Tax Assessment Rolls for Kerr County, Texas," 1888, p. 2, line 1, and 1891, p. 1, line 38, State Archives.
4. Charles Apelt, *The Armadillo*.
5. Kerr County Tax Assessor, "Tax Assessment Rolls for Kerr County, Texas," 1898, p. 1, lines 36–37, State Archives.
6. L. A. Wilke, "A Farmer's Shell Game," *Farm and Ranch* 47 (January 7, 1928): 4, 15.
7. Charles Apelt, *History of the Armadillo*, p. 3.
8. Edward R. Kalmbach to R. O. Farra, Highlands, Texas, June 10,

1937, U.S. Fish and Wildlife Service, General Correspondence, 1890–1944, Predatory Animals: Armadillos to Weasels, Box 551, Record Group 22, National Archives (hereafter cited as U.S. Fish and Wildlife Service, Predatory Animals).

9. Hart Stilwell, "'Protective Shell' for Armadillo Farm," *San Antonio Light*, March 13, 1967.

10. Apelt, *The Armadillo*, p. 3.

11. Ibid., pp. 11–19, 21.

12. John K. Strecker, "The Extension of the Range of the Nine-Banded Armadillo," *Journal of Mammalogy* 7 (1926): 208.

13. Newman, "Natural History," p. 515; Valgene Lehmann, "Armadillo Investigations" (notes from a 1939 survey).

14. Apelt, *The Armadillo*, p. 3.

15. Sam Kindrick, "Armadillos: A Cash Crop," *San Antonio Express/News*, October 27, 1963.

16. Burgess H. Scott, "'Dillo Ranching," *Ford Times* 39 (March 1947): 7–11; Edward R. Kalmbach, *The Armadillo: Its Relation to Agriculture and Game*, pp. 55–56.

17. Newman, "Natural History," pp. 514–515; Dennis A. Meritt, "Edentate Diets: 1. Armadillos," *Laboratory of Animal Science* 23 (1973): 540–542.

18. Charles Apelt, *A Mother Armadillo*; Kindrick, "Armadillos: A Cash Crop."

19. Scott, "'Dillo Ranching," p. 7.

20. Wick Fowler, "Catching Armadillo for Dinner Is Ticklish Task," *Dallas Morning News*, December 14, 1947; Frank X. Tolbert, "Can't Keep 'Em on Armadillo Farm," ibid., April 14, 1955. Tax records for Bell County reported a J. Y. M. Dowdy of Salado, Texas, who, in 1953, owned 70 acres; he does not appear in the tax rolls for 1956; see Bell County Tax Assessor, "Tax Assessment Rolls for Bell County, Texas," 1953, vol. 1, p. 242, lines 19–20, and 1956, p. 285, line 11, State Archives.

21. Floyd Potter, Texas Parks and Wildlife, personal communication, February 16, 1981.

22. Unless otherwise noted, details about the activities attributed to Sam Lewis and the World Armadillo Breeders and Racers Association are from an interview with Lewis in San Angelo, April 23, 1981.

23. "Armadillos Soaring toward Peking Zoo as Texas-Sized Gift," *Austin American-Statesman*, December 6, 1980.

24. L. C. Whitehead to Chief, Bureau of Biological Survey, May 20, 1929, U.S. Fish and Wildlife Service, Predatory Animals; Stanley

P. Young, in charge of economic investigations, BBS, to White-head, May 25, 1929, ibid.

25. L. C. Whitehead to Chief, Bureau of Biological Survey, July 15, 1930, U.S. Fish and Wildlife Service, Predatory Animals.

26. C. R. Landon to Chief, Bureau of Biological Survey, February 13, 1933, U.S. Fish and Wildlife Service, Predatory Animals.

27. William L. McAtee to William J. Tucker, February 25, 1933, U.S. Fish and Wildlife Service, Predatory Animals; Tucker to McAtee, March 24, 1933, ibid.

28. Tucker to McAtee, March 24, 1933.

29. Edward R. Kalmbach, "Report of a Field Study of the Armadillo in Texas, May 17–June 29, 1933," p. 7, in "Report on Rodent Control Operations in Texas," by L. C. Whitehead, U.S. Fish and Wildlife Service, Reports of Operations, 1915–1949, Record Group 22, National Archives.

30. Ibid., p. 5.

31. Ibid., pp. 7–8, 10–11.

32. Kalmbach, *The Armadillo*, p. 46.

33. U.S. Fish and Wildlife Service, Division of Wildlife Services, "Armadillos and Their Control," pamphlet, and office memorandum, February 8, 1960, General Correspondence, Armadillo Control, Record Group 22, National Archives.

34. Frank X. Tolbert, "Town Beset by Armadillos," *Dallas Morning News*, April 19, 1955.

35. Frank X. Tolbert, "Armadillo Now a 'Household Pest,'" *Dallas Morning News*, September 19, 1961.

36. Patricia A. Chamberlain, "Armadillos: Problems and Control," in *Proceedings, Ninth Vertebrate Pest Conference*, ed. Jerry P. Clark, pp. 162–169.

37. "Armadillos Attack Suburban Lawns," *San Antonio Express/News*, September 26, 1982; "Shortage of Armadillos Axes 'World Olympics,'" *Austin American-Statesman*, May 7, 1982.

38. J. Frank Dobie, "Hoover Hogs," *Frontier Times* 36 (1961): 32; Victor B. Fain, "Dots and Dashes," *Daily Sentinel* (Nacogdoches), October 11, 1982.

39. Vernon Bailey, *Biological Survey of Texas*, p. 53; Kalmbach, *The Armadillo*, p. 55.

40. Kalmbach, *The Armadillo*, p. 55 (quotation); Lehmann, "Armadillo Investigations"; H. A. Clapp, "Armadillo Meat Is Delicious," *Farm and Ranch* 47, no. 7 (1928): 5; Bob Gray, "Armadillo Barbecue Is East Texas Delicacy," *Houston Post*, October 28, 1958.

41. Kalmbach, *The Armadillo*, p. 55; Valgene Lehmann, personal

communication, January 19, 1983; Henry S. Fitch, Phil Goodrum, and Coleman Newman, "The Armadillo in the Southeastern United States," *Journal of Mammalogy* 33 (1952): 33; Frank Weaker, personal communication, March 12, 1981; C. R. Wenger, "The Amazing Armadillo," *Arkansas Game and Fish* 9 (Winter 1977): 8–10.

42. Kathryn Apelt Jorns, interview, Austin, October 9, 1980.
43. Frank X. Tolbert, "Centerville Chef's Armadillo Cookery," *Dallas Morning News*, December 13, 1969; idem, "Armadillo Breeders Association Attacked, Defeated," ibid., July 6, 1968; Nat Henderson, "Johnson City Loves Lovers of Wild Game," *Austin American-Statesman*, November 16, 1982.
44. Texas Folklore Society, "Big Thicket Balladry," in *Texas Folksongs*, p. 24; John C. Meyers, "The Mystery of the Five Graves," in *The Golden Log*, p. 53.
45. Frank X. Tolbert, "Armadillo Touted as 'State Beast,'" *Dallas Morning News*, October 31, 1968; R. H. Baker, "Fur Bearers Make Tasty Tidbits," *Texas Game and Fish* 2 (1944): 14–15; I. Hiller, "It's Become a Texan," *Texas Parks and Wildlife* 40, no. 1 (1982): 2–7; Hermes Nye, "A Treatise on the Frequently and Unjustifiably Maligned Armadillo," *Texas Parade* 36 (August 1975): 31; Frank X. Tolbert, "Armadillo Diet Takes Off Too Much Weight," *Dallas Morning News*, November 27, 1969.
46. U.S. Fish and Wildlife Service, Division of Wildlife Services, "Armadillos and Their Control," p. 3.
47. H. H. Newman and J. Thomas Patterson, "The Limits of Hereditary Control in Armadillo Quadruplets: A Study of Blastogenic Variation," *Journal of Morphology* 22 (1911): 855–926 (quotations, p. 861).
48. H. H. Newman and J. Thomas Patterson, "A Case of Normal Identical Quadruplets in the Nine-Banded Armadillo and Its Bearing on the Problems of Identical Twins and Sex Determination," *Biological Bulletin* 18 (1909): 181–187; Eleanor E. Storrs, "The Astonishing Armadillo," *National Geographic* 161 (1982): 820–830.
49. Storrs, "The Astonishing Armadillo," p. 820; Chamberlain, "Armadillos," p. 164.
50. Frank Weaker, personal communication, March 12, 1981.
51. Waldemar F. Kirchheimer, "HD Vaccines and Armadillos," *Star* 41 (March–April 1982): 12; Meny Bergel, "Leprosy (Hansen's Disease) Is Not an Infectious Disease," ibid. 41 (January–February 1982): 14.

52. Chapman H. Binford, Wayne M. Meyers and Gerald P. Walsh, "Leprosy," *Journal of the American Medical Association* 247 (1982): 2283–2292; "Hansen's Disease," in *Reported Morbidity and Mortality in Texas: 1981 Annual Summary*, Vol. 4, ed. Jan Pelosi, pp. 10–11; Gerald P. Walsh, personal communication, March 4, 1984.

53. G. H. Faget, R. C. Pogge, F. A. Johansen, et al., "The Promin Treatment of Leprosy: A Progress Report," *Public Health Report* 58 (1943): 1728–1741.

54. Eleanor E. Storrs, "The Nine-Banded Armadillo: A Model for Leprosy and Other Biomedical Research," *International Journal of Leprosy* 39 (1971): 703–714; Wayne M. Meyers et al., "Naturally Acquired Leprosy-like Disease in the Nine-Banded Armadillo (*Dasypus novemcinctus*): Reactions in Leprosy Patients to the Lepromins Prepared from Naturally Infected Armadillos," *Journal of the Reticuloendothelial Society* 22 (1977): 369–375; Waldemar F. Kirchheimer, "Lepromin—Its History, Preparation, and Use in HD Control," *The Star* 39 (January–February, 1980): 5.

55. Kirchheimer, "HD Vaccines," p. 12.

56. Gerald P. Walsh et al., "Leprosy—a Zoonosis," *Leprosy Review* 52 (1981), Supplement, Symposium on the Epidemiology of Leprosy, Galo, Norway, pp. 77–83; Jerome H. Smith et al., "Prevalence of Leprosy in Wild Armadillos of the Texas Gulf Coast," Paper at Tropical Medicine Meeting, Cleveland, Ohio, November 8–12, 1982; Gerald P. Walsh et al., "Naturally Acquired Leprosy-like Disease in the Nine-Banded Armadillo (*Dasypus novemcinctus*): Recent Epizootiologic Findings," *Journal of the Reticuloendothelial Society* 22 (1977): 363–367.

57. T. Imaeda, L. Barksdale, and W. F. Kirchheimer, "Genome Size and Homology of Deoxyribonucleic Acids of Mycobacteria," in *Proceedings of the Sixteenth Joint Conference on Tuberculosis, the U.S.-Japan Cooperative Medical Science Program*, pp. 300–310.

58. T. F. Davey and R. J. W. Rees, "The Nasal Discharge in Leprosy: Clinical and Bacteriological Aspects," *Leprosy Review* 45 (1974): 121–134; Gerald P. Walsh, personal communication, March 4, 1984.

59. Binford, Meyers, and Walsh, "Leprosy," p. 2285; Harley F. Freiberger and H. Hugh Fudenberg, "An Appetite for Armadillo," *Hospital Practice* 16 (June 1981): 141–144 (quotation, p. 144); Lee R. Lumpkin, Gary F. Cox, and John E. Wolf, "Leprosy in Five Armadillo Hunters," *Journal of the American Academy of Dermatology* 9 (1983): 899–903.

60. Walsh et al., "Leprosy—a zoonosis," pp. 79–80.

61. Ibid., p. 82 (quotations).

62. "'Dillos Spark Health Debate," *Austin American-Statesman*, September 8, 1980; Gerald P. Walsh to F. B. S. Antram, Research Assistant, IUCN/SSC Specialist Group, London, April 24, 1980, U.S. Fish and Wildlife Service, Office of Scientific Authority; Barry Hafkin, personal communication, Austin, January 21, 1982.

63. Vernon Bailey, "Mammals of the Lone Star State," *Nature Magazine* 16 (1930): 363–365, 386.

64. Roy Bedichek, *Adventures with a Texas Naturalist*, pp. 59–60, 63.

65. Cheryl Coggins, "Ice-Cold Armadillo: A Hot Item," *Austin American-Statesman*, March 21, 1982.

66. U.S. Fish and Wildlife Service, News Release, November 9, 1982.

4. THE ARMADILLO IN POPULAR CULTURE

1. National Wildlife Federation, *Official Birds, Mammals, Trees, Flowers, Insects, and Fish of the U.S., Territories, and Possessions, Revised*.

2. Unless otherwise noted, details about the World Armadillo Breeders and Racers Association and other activities attributed to Sam Lewis are from an interview with Lewis in San Angelo, April 23, 1981.

3. Carolyn S. Miller, "Armadillo Crazy," *Texas Highways* 20 (February 1982): 16; "Dilly of an Armadillo Race Hits New Braunfels," *Austin American-Statesman*, August 22, 1981.

4. Bob Trott, "Jaycees Plan Excursion to Catch Own Armadillos," *Mid-Valley Town Crier* (Weslaco), January 3, 1982.

5. For an overview, see Craig Hattersley, "Whither the Armadillo? And Where From?" *Texas Observer* 72 (December 26, 1980): 6–12.

6. Hattersley, "Whither the Armadillo?" p. 6 (quotation); Cindy Widner, "Goin' Home with the Armadillo," *Daily Texan*, April 20, 1980.

7. KTBC-TV, "The Rise and Fall of the Armadillo World Headquarters" (film), February 27, 1981.

8. Ed Ward, "Thanks for the Memories," *Austin American-Statesman*, January 2, 1981 (quotation).

9. Hermes Nye, "A Treatise on the Frequently and Unjustifiably Maligned Armadillo," *Texas Parade* 36 (August 1975): 29–31 (quotation, p. 30); Russel Middleton and O'Neil Provost, "Armadillos Come from Daydreams: A Closer Look at Jim Franklin," *Austin People Today* (November 1974), pp. 16–17.

10. "Armadillo Man," *New Yorker*, December 11, 1971, pp. 41–42 (quotation, p. 41).

11. *Texas Ranger* "Armadillo Man," 80 (September 1965), 2: p. 42.

12. Nye, "A Treatise," p. 30.

13. Ward, "Thanks for the Memories."

14. Ed Ward, "When the Walls Tumble, the Art Won't Crumble," *Austin American-Statesman*, November 28, 1980.

15. John Kelso, "'Dillo Decor Sold to Tune of $45,000," *Austin American-Statesman*, January 11, 1981.

16. Survey form for Historic Landmark Inventory, City of Austin, May 13, 1980, p. 2, in Armadillo File, Travis County Collection, Austin Public Library; Gladys Candy, "Austin Club Bankrupt," *Billboard*, January 29, 1977.

17. Kelso, "'Dillo Decor Sold" (quotation); Patrick Brown, "Workers Discover 'Dillo Stash," *Daily Texan*, February 4, 1981.

18. John Kelso, "'Dillo Hands Stay in Tune," *Austin American-Statesman*, December 11, 1982.

19. Jane Ulrich, "A Texas Christmas," *Austin American-Statesman*, December 1, 1980; "Stuffed 'Dillo Takes Place of Teddy Bear," ibid., May 10, 1981.

20. Robert Heard, interview with Eddie Wilson, June 26, 1974, tape no. 108, Travis County Collection, Austin Public Library; Anne Pearson, "Goodbye Lone Star 'Dillo," *San Antonio Express / News*, April 13, 1983.

21. For instances of the range of armadilliana, consult *Austin American-Statesman*, February 26, August 13, and December 26, 1982; and *The Armadillo: Arts, Entertainment, and Living in the Rio Grande Valley* (a Brownsville weekly newspaper with a circulation of 40,000), October 20, 1982.

22. "Time Out," *Austin American-Statesman*, January 10, 1981; Amy Mashberg and Melinda Machado, "Capitol 10,000 Draws Thousands," *Daily Texan*, March 23, 1981; "Get Ready to Enter," *Austin American-Statesman*, January 8, 1983; Dick Stanley, "Fleet Armadillo Paces Field of Novelty Racers," ibid., March 19, 1984.

23. Jim Gibbs, "Austin Trolleys Begin Routes," *Daily Texan*, March 20, 1984 (quotation); Pete Szilagyi, "Catch a 'Dillo' Begins Downtown Run," *Austin American-Statesman*, March 20, 1984.

24. "Oak Creek Joins Hands with Legislators to Name a State Mammal," *Spring Times* (Spring Independent School District, Houston), Summer 1979.

25. Carole Allen and S. Childers, promoters of "Armadillo in '81," personal communication, Austin, April 2 and 16, 1981.

26. Notes from House debate on HCR 53, April 16, 1981; "In Praise of 'Dillos," *Austin American-Statesman*, April 17, 1981; Dinah Wisenberg, "House Passes 'Dillo Resolution," *Daily Texan*, April 17, 1981.

27. "'Dillo Resolution Might Get Grounded," *Austin American-Statesman*, May 28, 1981.

28. Ibid.; "In Praise of 'Dillos."

29. Bill Cryer, "Ogg Itches to Finally Call 'Dillo a Mascot," *Austin American-Statesman*, October 2, 1981.

30. Wayne King, "The Great Texas Armadillo Hunt: Tracking Down a Shy Guest of Honor," *New York Times*, December 7, 1982.

5. ARMADILLOS FOREVER

1. John James Audubon and John Bachman, *Quadrupeds of North America* 3: 224–225.

2. Stephen R. Humphrey, "Zoogeography of the Nine-Banded Armadillo, (*Dasypus novemcinctus*) in the United States," *BioScience* 24 (1974): 457–462.

3. Ibid.; Albert E. Sanders, "Order Edentata," in *An Annotated Checklist of the Biota of the Coastal Zone of South Carolina*, ed. Richard G. Zingmark, p. 299.

4. William K. Clark, "Ecological Life History of the Armadillo in the Eastern Edwards Plateau Region" (M.A. thesis, University of Texas at Austin, 1949), pp. 35–39.

5. Ralph M. Wetzel and Edgardo Mondolfi, "The Subgenera and Species of Long-Nosed Armadillos, Genus *Dasypus* L.," in *Vertebrate Ecology in the Northern Neotropics*, ed. John F. Eisenberg, pp. 51–53.

6. David H. Greegor, "Renal Capabilities of an Argentine Desert Armadillo," *Journal of Mammalogy* 56 (1975): 626–632.

7. Vernon Bailey, "Mammals of the Lone Star State," *Nature Magazine* 16 (1930): 363–365, 386.

8. Henry S. Fitch, Phil Goodrum and Coleman Newman, "The Armadillo in the Southeastern United States," *Journal of Mammalogy* 33 (1952): 21–27.

Bibliography

PUBLISHED MATERIAL

Allen, Joel Asaph. "On Mammals Collected in Bexar County and Vicinity, Texas, by Mr. H. P. Attwater, with Field Notes by the Collector." *Bulletin of the American Museum of Natural History* 8 (April 1896): 47–80.

Apelt, Carl (Charles). *Armadillo Korbchen.* German-language brochure promoting the Apelt Armadillo Co. Comfort, Tex., n.d.

Apelt, Charles. *The Armadillo.* Comfort, Tex.: Apelt Armadillo Co., n.d.

———. *History of the Armadillo.* Brochure. N.p.: Apelt Armadillo Co., n.d.

———. *A Mother Armadillo.* Brochure. Comfort, Tex.: Apelt Armadillo Co., n.d.

The Armadillo: Arts, Entertainment and Living in the Rio Grande Valley. Weekly newspaper. Brownsville, Tex.

"Armadillo Man." *New Yorker*, December 11, 1971, pp. 41–42.

"Armadillo Provides Advances in Leprosy Studies." *BioScience* 24 (1974): 746.

"Armadillos: A Cash Crop." *San Antonio Express/News*, October 27, 1963.

"Armadillos Attack Suburban Lawns." *San Antonio Express/News*, September 26, 1982.

"Armadillos Soaring toward Peking Zoo as Texas-Sized Gift." *Austin American-Statesman*, December 6, 1980.

Armstrong, D. M., and J. K. Jones, Jr. "Mammals from the Mexican State of Sinaloa." *Journal of Mammalogy* 52 (1971): 747–757.

Audubon, John James, and John Bachman. *Quadrupeds of North America.*, vol. 3. New York: V. G. Audubon, 1854.

Bailey, H. H. "The Armadillo in Florida and How It Reached There." *Journal of Mammalogy* 5 (1924): 264–265.

Bailey, Vernon. *Biological Survey of Texas.* North American Fauna, no. 25. Washington, D.C.: U.S. Government Printing Office, 1905.

123

BIBLIOGRAPHY

————. *Mammals of New Mexico.* North American Fauna, no. 53. Washington, D.C.: U.S. Government Printing Office, 1931.

————. "Mammals of the Lone Star State." *Nature Magazine* 16 (1930): 363–365, 386.

Baker, A. B. "The Nine-Banded Armadillo." *Science*, n.s. 4 (1896): 52.

Baker, R. H. "Fur Bearers Make Tasty Tidbits." *Texas Game and Fish* 2 (1944): 14–15.

Baker, R. H., and J. K. Greer. "Notes on Oaxacan Mammals." *Journal of Mammalogy* 41 (1960): 413–415.

Bedichek, Roy. *Adventures with a Texas Naturalist.* Austin: University of Texas Press, 1961.

Bennett, Charles F., Jr. "Cultural Animal Geography: An Inviting Field of Research." *Professional Geographer* 12 (1960): 12–14.

Bergel, Meny. "Leprosy (Hansen's Disease) Is Not an Infectious Disease." *Star* 41 (January–February 1982): 14.

Best, Troy L., Barbara Hoditschek, and Howard H. Thomas. "Foods of Coyotes (*Canis latrans*) in Oklahoma." *Southwestern Naturalist* 26 (1981): 67–69.

Binford, Chapman H., Wayne M. Meyers, and Gerald P. Walsh. "Leprosy." *Journal of the American Medical Association* 247 (1982): 2283–2292.

Black, J. D. "Another Arkansas Armadillo." *Journal of Mammalogy* 25 (1944): 415.

Blair, W. Frank. "Biotic Provinces of Texas." *Texas Journal of Science* 2 (1950): 73–117.

————. "The Nine-Banded Armadillo in Northeastern Oklahoma." *Journal of Mammalogy* 17 (1936): 293–294.

Bracht, Viktor. *Texas in 1848.* Translated by C. F. Schmidt. San Antonio: Naylor, 1931.

Brown, Patrick. "Workers Discover 'Dillo Stash." *Daily Texan*, February 4, 1981.

Buchanan, G. D. "The Current Range of the Armadillo *Dasypus novemcinctus mexicanus* in the United States." *Texas Journal of Science* 10 (1958): 349–351.

Buchanan, G. D., and Roy V. Talmage. "The Geographical Distribution of the Armadillo in the United States." *Texas Journal of Science* 6 (1954): 142–150.

Burns, T. A., and E. B. Waldrip. "Body Temperature and Electrocardiographic Data for the Nine-Banded Armadillo (*Dasypus novemcinctus*)." *Journal of Mammalogy* 52 (1971): 472–473.

Candy, Gladys. "Austin Club Bankrupt." *Billboard*, January 29, 1977.

Chamberlain, Patricia A. "Armadillos: Problems and Control." In *Pro-*

ceedings, Ninth Vertebrate Pest Conference, edited by Jerry P. Clark. Davis: University of California, 1980.

Clapp, H. A. "Armadillo Meat Is Delicious." *Farm and Ranch* 47, no. 7 (1928): 5.

Clark, William K. "Ecological Life History of the Armadillo in the Eastern Edwards Plateau Region." *American Midland Naturalist* 46 (1951): 337–358.

Cleveland, A. G. "The Current Geographic Distribution of the Armadillo in the United States." *Texas Journal of Science* 22 (1970): 90–92.

Cockrum, E. L. *Mammals of Kansas.* University of Kansas Publications, Museum of Natural History, vol. 7, no. 1. Lawrence: University of Kansas Press, 1952.

Coggins, Cheryl. "Ice-Cold Armadillo: A Hot Item." *Austin American-Statesman,* March 21, 1982.

Cope, Edward Drinker. "On the Zoological Position of Texas." *Bulletin of the U.S. National Museum* 17 (1880): 1–51.

Crosby, Gilbert T. "Spread of the Cattle Egret in the Western Hemisphere." *Bird Banding* 43 (July 1972): 205–212.

Cryer, Bill. "Ogg Itches to Finally Call 'Dillo a Mascot." *Austin American-Statesman,* October 2, 1981.

"The Dallas Shell Game: World's Top Armadillo to Be Selected Today." *Wall Street Journal,* October 18, 1968.

Davey, T. F., and R. J. W. Rees. "The Nasal Discharge in Leprosy: Clinical and Bacteriological Aspects." *Leprosy Review* 45 (1974): 121–134.

Davis, William B. *The Mammals of Texas.* Austin: Texas Parks and Wildlife, 1974.

———, and R. J. Russell. "Mammals of the Mexican State of Morelos." *Journal of Mammalogy* 35 (1954): 63–80.

Dellinger, S. C., and J. D. Black. "Notes on Arkansas Mammals." *Journal of Mammalogy* 21 (1940): 187–191.

Dice, L. R. *The Biotic Provinces of North America.* Ann Arbor: University of Michigan Press, 1943.

"'Dillo Resolution Might Get Grounded." *Austin American-Statesman,* May 28, 1981.

"'Dillos Go under Knife." *Daily Texan,* November 19, 1980.

"'Dillos Spark Health Debate." *Austin American-Statesman,* September 8, 1980.

"Dilly of an Armadillo Race Hits New Braunfels." *Austin American-Statesman,* August 22, 1981.

Dobie, J. Frank. "The Armadillo Gets the Milk." *Austin American-Statesman,* November 16, 1958.

125

————. "Hoover Hogs." *Frontier Times* 36 (1961): 32.

Dumble, Edwin T. "The Armadillo (*Tatusia peba*) in Texas." *American Naturalist* 26 (1892): 72.

Eisenberg, John F. "Observation on the Nest Building Behavior of Armadillos." *Proceedings of the Zoological Society of London* 137 (1961): 323.

Elton, Charles S. *Animal Ecology.* New York: October House, 1966.

————. *The Ecology of Invasions by Animals and Plants.* London: Chapman and Hall, 1958.

Everett, Donald E. *San Antonio: The Flavor of Its Past, 1845–1898.* San Antonio: Trinity University Press, 1975.

Faget, G. H., R. C. Pogge, F. A. Johansen, et al. "The Promin Treatment of Leprosy: A Progress Report." *Public Health Report* 58 (1943): 1728–1741.

Fain, Victor B. "Dots and Dashes." *Daily Sentinel* (Nacogdoches), October 11, 1982.

Fitch, Henry S., Phil Goodrum, and Coleman Newman. "The Armadillo in the Southeastern United States." *Journal of Mammalogy* 33 (1952): 21–37.

"4 Armadillos from West Texas Arrive in Peking." *Austin American-Statesman*, December 9, 1980.

Fowler, Wick. "Catching Armadillo for Dinner Is Ticklish Task." *Dallas Morning News*, December 14, 1947.

Freiberger, Harley F., and H. Hugh Fudenberg. "An Appetite for Armadillo." *Hospital Practice* 16 (June 1981): 141–144.

Gardner, M. C. "Another Oklahoma Armadillo." *Journal of Mammalogy* 29 (1948): 76.

George, Wilma. *Animal Geography.* London: Heinemann, 1962.

"Geosource Inc. Ships Armadillos to Peking Zoo." *Wall Street Journal,* December 5, 1980.

"Get Ready to Enter." *Austin American-Statesman*, January 8, 1983.

Getz, L. L. "New Locality Records of Some Kansas Mammals." *Journal of Mammalogy* 42 (1961): 282–283.

Gibbs, Jim. "Austin Trolleys Begin Routes." *Daily Texan*, March 20, 1984.

Glass, B. P., and A. F. Halloran. "The Small Mammals of the Wichita Mountains Wildlife Refuge, Oklahoma." *Journal of Mammalogy.* 42 (1961): 234–239.

Golley, F. B. *Mammals of Georgia.* Athens, Ga.: University of Georgia Press, 1962.

Gray, Bob. "Armadillo Barbecue Is East Texas Delicacy." *Houston Post*, October 28, 1958.

Greegor, David H. "Renal Capabilities of an Argentine Desert Armadillo." *Journal of Mammalogy* 56 (1975): 626–632.

Hahn, D. E. "The Nine-Banded Armadillo, *Dasypus novemcinctus*, in Colorado." *Southwestern Naturalist* 11 (1966): 303.

"Hansen's Disease." In *Reported Morbidity and Mortality in Texas: 1981 Annual Summary*, vol. 4, edited by Jan Pelosi, pp. 10–11. Austin: Texas Department of Health, 1982.

Hattersley, Craig. "Whither the Armadillo? And Where From?" *Texas Observer* 72 (December 26, 1980): 6–12.

Henderson, Nat. "Johnson City Loves Lovers of Wild Game." *Austin American-Statesman*, November 16, 1982.

Hendricks, L. Joseph. "Observation of Armadillo in East-Central New Mexico." *Journal of Mammalogy* 44 (1963): 581.

Hill, E. O. "The Artful Armadillo." *Nature Magazine* 20 (November 1932): 218–219.

Hiller, I. "It's Become a Texan." *Texas Parks and Wildlife* 40, no. 1 (1982): 2–7.

Hollister, N. "The Systematic Name of the Texas Armadillo." *Journal of Mammalogy* 6 (1925): 60.

Humphrey, Stephen R. "Zoogeography of the Nine-Banded Armadillo (*Dasypus novemcinctus*) in the United States." *BioScience* 24 (1974): 457–462.

Imaeda, T., L. Barksdale, and W. F. Kirchheimer. "Genome Size and Homology of Deoxyribonucleic Acids of Mycobacteria." In *Proceedings of the Sixteenth Joint Conference on Tuberculosis, the U.S.-Japan Cooperative Medical Science Program, National Institute of Health, Bethesda, Maryland, November 16–17, 1981*, pp. 300–310.

"In Praise of 'Dillos." *Austin American-Statesman*, April 17, 1981.

Johansen, Kjell. "Temperature Regulation in the Nine-Banded Armadillo (*Dasypus novemcinctus mexicanus*)." *Physiological Zoology* 34 (1961): 126–144.

Kalmbach, Edward R. *The Armadillo: Its Relation to Agriculture and Game*. Austin: Texas Game, Fish, and Oyster Commission, 1943.

Kelso, John. "'Dillo Decor Sold to Tune of $45,000." *Austin American-Statesman*, January 11, 1981.

———. "'Dillo Hands Stay in Tune," *Austin American-Statesman*, December 11, 1982.

Kindrick, Sam. "Armadillos: A Cash Crop." *San Antonio Express/News*, October 27, 1963.

King, Wayne. "The Great Texas Armadillo Hunt: Tracking Down a Shy Guest of Honor." *New York Times*, December 7, 1982.

BIBLIOGRAPHY

Kirchheimer, Waldemar F. "HD Vaccines and Armadillos." *Star* 41 (March–April 1982): 12.

―――. "Lepromin―Its History, Preparation, and Use in HD Control." *Star* 39 (January–February 1980): 5.

――― "Leprosy Vaccine Trials to Begin Soon." *Science* 215 (1982): 1083–1086.

―――. "The Testing of Purified Armadillo-Derived *M. leprae* in Man." *Star* 41 (May–June 1982): 15.

Layne, James N., and Debbie Glover. "Home Range of the Armadillo in Florida." *Journal of Mammalogy* 58 (1977): 411–413.

Lehmann, Valgene. *Forgotten Legions: Sheep in the Rio Grande Plain of Texas.* El Paso: Texas Western Press, 1969.

Linsalata, Mark. "And You Thought Armadillos Were Cute." *San Antonio Light*, January 30, 1983.

Long, John L. *Introduced Birds of the World.* New York: Universe Books, 1981.

Loughmiller, Campbell and Lynn, eds. *Big Thicket Legacy.* Austin: University of Texas Press, 1977.

Lumpkin, Lee R., Gary F. Cox, and John E. Wolf. "Leprosy in Five Armadillo Hunters." *Journal of the American Academy of Dermatology* 9 (1983): 899–903.

Lundy, Benjamin F. 1969. *The Life, Travels, and Opinions of Benjamin Lundy.* New York: Negro Universities Press, 1969.

McBee, Karen, and Robert J. Baker. "Dasypus novemcinctus." *Mammalian Species* (American Society of Mammalogists), no. 162 (1982): 1–9.

Mashberg, Amy, and Melinda Machado. "Capitol 10,000 Draws Thousands." *Daily Texan*, March 23, 1981.

Meritt, Dennis A. "Edentate Diets: 1. Armadillos." *Laboratory of Animal Science* 23 (1973): 540–542.

Meyers, John C. "The Mystery of the Five Graves." In *The Golden Log.* Dallas: Southern Methodist University, 1962.

Meyers, Wayne M., et al. "Naturally Acquired Leprosy-like Disease in the Nine-Banded Armadillo (*Dasypus novemcinctus*): Reactions in Leprosy Patients to the Lepromins Prepared from Naturally Infected Armadillos." *Journal of the Reticuloendothelial Society* 22 (1977): 369–375.

Middleton, Russel, and O'Neil Provost. "Armadillos Come from Daydreams: A Closer Look at Jim Franklin." *Austin People Today*, November 1974, pp. 16–17.

Miller, Carolyn S. "Armadillo Crazy." *Texas Highways* 20 (February 1982): 16.

Moeller, Walburga. "Edentates." In *Grzimek's Animal Life Encyclopedia* 11: 149–166. New York: Van Nostrand Reinhold, 1975.

Moore, J. C. "Mammals from Welaka, Putnam County, Florida." *Journal of Mammalogy* 27 (1946): 49–59.

National Wildlife Federation. *Official Birds, Mammals, Trees, Flowers, Insects, and Fish of the U.S., Territories, and Possessions, Revised.* Washington, D.C., 1978.

"Native Texan." Advertisement for Stelfox and Co. *Austin American-Statesman,* February 26, 1981.

Neill, Wilfred T. "The Spread of the Armadillo in Florida." *Ecology* 33 (1952): 282–284.

Newman, Coleman C., and Rollin H. Baker. "Armadillo Eats Young Rabbits." *Journal of Mammalogy* 23 (1942): 450.

Newman, H. H. "The Natural History of the Nine-Banded Armadillo of Texas." *American Naturalist* 47 (1913): 513–539.

Newman, H. H., and J. Thomas Patterson. "A Case of Normal Identical Quadruplets in the Nine-Banded Armadillo and Its Bearing on the Problems of Identical Twins and Sex Determination." *Biological Bulletin* 18 (1909): 181–187.

———. "The Limits of Hereditary Control in Armadillo Quadruplets: A Study of Blastogenic Variation." *Journal of Morphology* 22 (1911): 855–926.

Nye, Hermes. "A Treatise on the Frequently and Unjustifiably Maligned Armadillo." *Texas Parade* 36 (August 1975): 29–31.

"Oak Creek Joins Hands with Legislators to Name a State Mammal." *Spring Times* (Spring Independent School District, Houston), Summer 1979.

Pearson, Anne. "Goodbye, Lone Star 'Dillo." *San Antonio Express/News,* April 13, 1983.

Sanders, Albert E. "Order Edentata." In *An Annotated Checklist of the Biota of the Coastal Zone of South Carolina,* edited by Richard G. Zingmark. Columbia: University of South Carolina Press, 1978.

Schaefer, Jack W. *An American Bestiary.* Boston: Houghton Mifflin, 1975.

Schmidly, David J. *The Mammals of Trans-Pecos Texas.* College Station: Texas A&M University Press, 1977.

Schwartz, C. W., and E. R. Schwartz. *The Wild Mammals of Missouri.* Columbia: University of Missouri Press, 1959.

Scott, Burgess H. "'Dillo Ranching." *Ford Times* 39 (March 1947): 7–11.

Sealander, J. A. "A Provisional Checklist and Key to the Mammals of Arkansas." *American Midland Naturalist* 56 (1956): 257–296.

"Shortage of Armadillos Axes 'World Olympics.'" *Austin American-Statesman*, May 7, 1982.

Stanley, Dick. "Fleet Armadillo Paces Field of Novelty Racers." *Austin American-Statesman*, March 19, 1984.

Stilwell, Hart. "'Protective Shell' for Armadillo Farm." *San Antonio Light*, March 13, 1967.

Storrs, Eleanor E. "The Astonishing Armadillo." *National Geographic* 161 (1982): 820–830.

———. "The Nine-Banded Armadillo: A Model for Leprosy and Other Biomedical Research." *International Journal of Leprosy* 39 (1971): 703–714.

Strecker, John K. "Notes on the Fauna of a Portion of the Canyon Region of Northwestern Texas." *Baylor Bulletin* 13 (1910): 21–22.

———. "The Extension of the Range of the Nine-Banded Armadillo." *Journal of Mammalogy* 7 (1926): 206–210.

———. "The Nine-Banded Armadillo in Northeastern Louisiana." *Journal of Mammalogy* 9 (1928): 69–70.

———. "A Possible Albino Armadillo." *Journal of Mammalogy* 8 (1927): 60.

"Stuffed 'Dillo Takes Place of Teddy Bear." *Austin American-Statesman*, May 10, 1981.

Swepston, Danny. *The Status of the Armadillo in Texas.* Austin: Texas Parks and Wildlife Department, 1974.

Szilagyi, Pete. "Catch a 'Dillo' Begins Downtown Run." *Austin American-Statesman*, March, 20, 1984.

Taber, F. Wallace. "Contribution on the Life History and Ecology of the Nine-Banded Armadillo." *Journal of Mammalogy* 26 (1945): 211–226.

———. "Extension of the Range of the Armadillo." *Journal of Mammalogy* 20 (1939): 489–493.

Taylor, W. P. "Armadillos Abundant in Kerr County, Texas." *Journal of Mammalogy* 27 (1946): 273.

Texas Folklore Society. "Big Thicket Balladry." In *Texas Folksongs.* Austin, 1950.

Texas Ranger 80 (1965): 2.

"Time Out." *Austin American-Statesman*, January 10, 1981.

Tolbert, Frank X. "Armadillo Breeders Association Attacked, Defeated." *Dallas Morning News*, July 6, 1968.

———. "Armadillo Diet Takes Off Too Much Weight," *Dallas Morning News*, November 27, 1969.

———. "Armadillo Now a 'Household Pest.'" *Dallas Morning News*, September 19, 1961.

―――. "Armadillo Touted as 'State Beast.'" *Dallas Morning News*, October 31, 1968.

―――. "Can't Keep 'Em on Armadillo Farm." *Dallas Morning News*, April 14, 1955.

―――. "Centerville Chef's Armadillo Cookery." *Dallas Morning News*, December 13, 1969.

―――. "Town Beset by Armadillos." *Dallas Morning News*, April 19, 1955.

Trott, Bob. "Jaycees Plan Excursion to Catch Own Armadillos." *Mid-Valley Town Crier* (Weslaco), January 3, 1982.

Udvardy, Miklos D. F. *Dynamic Zoogeography*. New York: Van Nostrand Reinhold, 1969.

Ulrich, Jane. "A Texas Christmas." *Austin American-Statesman*, December 1, 1980.

U.S. Fish and Wildlife Service. "News Release." November 9, 1982.

Vaughan, Terry A. *Mammalogy*. Philadelphia: Saunders, 1972.

Walker, Ernest P. *Mammals of the World*, 3d ed., vol. 1. Baltimore: Johns Hopkins University Press, 1975.

Walsh, Gerald P., et al. "Leprosy―a zoonosis." *Leprosy Review* 52 (1981), Supplement, Symposium on the Epidemiology of Leprosy, Galo, Norway, pp. 77–83.

―――. "Naturally Acquired Leprosy-like Disease in the Nine-Banded Armadillo (*Dasypus novemcinctus*): Recent Epizootiologic Findings." *Journal of the Reticuloendothelial Society* 22 (1977): 363–367.

Ward, Ed. "When the Walls Tumble, the Art Won't Crumble." *Austin American-Statesman*, November 28, 1980.

―――. "Thanks for the Memories." *Austin American-Statesman*, January 2, 1981.

Wenger, C. R. "The Amazing Armadillo." *Arkansas Game and Fish* 9 (Winter 1977): 8–10.

Wetzel, Ralph M., and Edgardo Mondolfi. "The Subgenera and Species of Long-Nosed Armadillos, Genus *Dasypus* L." In *Vertebrate Ecology in the Northern Neotropics*, edited by John F. Eisenberg, pp. 43–63. Washington, D.C.: Smithsonian Institution Press, 1979.

Widner, Cindy. "Goin' Home with the Armadillo." *Daily Texan*, April 20, 1980.

Wilke, L. A. "A Farmer's Shell Game." *Farm and Ranch* 47, (January 7, 1928): 4, 15.

Wisenberg, Dinah. "House Passes 'Dillo Resolution." *Daily Texan*, April 17, 1981.

BIBLIOGRAPHY

UNPUBLISHED MATERIAL

Armadillo File. Travis County Collection, Austin Public Library. Austin.

Attwater, Henry P. Letter to Edward Preble, May 17, 1929. Record Unit 7252, Edward Alexander Preble Papers, Box 1, Folder 8. Smithsonian Institution Archives. Washington, D.C.

Bailey, Vernon. "Texas: Kerrville to Rock Springs, July 1–August 1, 1902." Record Unit 7176, U.S. Fish and Wildlife Service, Field Reports, Box 92, Folder 24. Smithsonian Institution Archives. Washington, D.C.

Bell County Tax Assessor. "Tax Assessment Rolls for Bell County, Texas," 1953, 1956. State Archives. Austin.

Clark, William K. "Ecological Life History of the Armadillo in the Eastern Edwards Plateau Region." M.A. thesis, University of Texas, 1949. Austin.

Heard, Robert. Interview with Eddie Wilson, June 26, 1974. Tape no. 108, Travis County Collection, Austin Public Library, Austin.

Kalmbach, Edward R. Letter to R. O. Farra, Highlands, Texas, June 10, 1937. U.S. Fish and Wildlife Service, General Correspondence, 1890–1944, Predatory Animals: Armadillos to Weasels, Box 551. Record Group 22, National Archives. Washington, D.C.

———. "Report of a Field Study of the Armadillo in Texas, May 17–June 29, 1933." In "Report on Rodent Control Operations in Texas," by L. C. Whitehead. U.S. Fish and Wildlife Service, Reports of Operations, 1915–1949. Record Group 22, National Archives. Washington, D.C.

Kerr County Tax Assessor. "Tax Assessment Rolls for Kerr County, Texas," 1888, 1891, 1898. State Archives. Austin.

KTBC-TV. "The Rise and Fall of the Armadillo World Headquarters" (film). February 27, 1981. Austin.

Landon, C. R. Letter to Chief, Bureau of Biological Survey, February 13, 1933. U.S. Fish and Wildlife Service, General Correspondence, 1890–1944, Predatory Animals: Armadillos to Weasels, Box 551. Record Group 22, National Archives. Washington, D.C.

Lehmann, Valgene. "Armadillo Investigations." Miscellaneous notes from a 1939 survey. Personal files of V. Lehmann.

Lloyd, William. "Mammals of the Lower Rio Grande." Special Reports, 1890. Record Unit 7176, U.S. Fish and Wildlife Service, Field Reports, Box 94, Folder 18. Smithsonian Institution Archives. Washington, D.C.

McAtee, William L. Letter to William J. Tucker, Executive Secretary, Texas Game, Fish, and Oyster Commission, February 25, 1933. U.S.

Fish and Wildlife Service, General Correspondence, 1890–1944, Predatory Animals: Armadillos to Weasels, Box 551. Record Group 22, National Archives. Washington, D.C.

Mitchell, J. D. Letter to Vernon Bailey, March 25, 1915. Record Unit 7176, U.S. Fish and Wildlife Service, Field Reports, Box 95, Folder, 7. Smithsonian Institution Archives. Washington, D.C.

Nesbitt, S. A., W. M. Hetrick, L. E. Williams, and D. H. Austin. "Foods of the Nine-Banded Armadillo in Florida." Florida Pittman-Robertson Project W-41-R. Gainesville(?): Florida Game and Fresh Water Commission, n.d. (17 pp., mimeo.)

Oberholser, Harry. "Texas: Laredo Mammals," May 1901. Record Group 7176, U.S. Fish and Wildlife Service, Field Reports, Box 95, Folder 16. Smithsonian Institution Archives. Washington, D.C.

Smith, Jerome H., et al. "Prevalence of Leprosy in Wild Armadillos of the Texas Gulf Coast." Paper presented at Tropical Medicine Meeting, Cleveland, Ohio, November 8–12, 1982.

Smithsonian Institution, "National Zoological Park Records, 1887–1965." General correspondence, 1899–1930, Animals Acquired: Armadillos–Beavers. Record Unit 74, Box 57, Folder 1. Smithsonian Institution Archives. Washington, D.C.

Texas House of Representatives. "House Concurrent Resolution No. 53." 67th Legislature. D. Henderson, sponsor. 1981.

Tucker, William J. Letter to William L. McAtee, March 24, 1933. U.S. Fish and Wildlife Service, General Correspondence, 1890–1944, Predatory Animals: Armadillos to Weasels, Box 551. Record Group 22, National Archives. Washington, D.C.

U.S. Fish and Wildlife Service, Division of Wildlife Services. "Armadillos and Their Control." General Correspondence, Armadillo Control. Record Group 22, National Archives. Washington, D.C.

———. General Correspondence, Wildlife Management, P-R Armadillo. Record Group 22, National Archives. Washington, D.C.

Walsh, Gerald P. Letter to F. B. S. Antram, Research Assistant, IUCN/SSC Specialist Group, London, April 24, 1980. U.S. Fish and Wildlife Service, Office of Scientific Authority. Washington, D.C.

Whitehead, L. C. Letter to Chief, Bureau of Biological Survey, May 20, 1929. U.S. Fish and Wildlife Service, General Correspondence, 1890–1944, Predatory Animals: Armadillos to Weasels, Box 551. Record Group 22, National Archives. Washington, D.C.

———. Letter to Chief, Bureau of Biological Survey, July 15, 1930. U.S. Fish and Wildlife Service, General Correspondence, 1890–1944, Predatory Animals: Armadillos to Weasels, Box 551. Record Group 22, National Archives. Washington, D.C.

BIBLIOGRAPHY

Young, Stanley P. Letter to L. C. Whitehead, May 25, 1929. U.S. Fish and Wildlife Service, General Correspondence, 1890–1944, Predatory Animals: Armadillos to Weasels, Box 551. Record Group 22, National Archives. Washington, D.C.